## HUMAN RESOURCE CERTIFICATION INSTITUTE

# CERTIFICATION GUIDE

Raymond B. Weinberg, CCP, SPHR

©1996 Human Resource Certification Institute
606 North Washington Street, Alexandria, Virginia 22314

*All rights reserved.* No part of this publication may be reproduced, stored in retrieval system, or transmitted in any form or by any means, electronic, mechanical, photocopying, recording or otherwise without the prior written permission of the copyright holder.

ISBN 0-939900-52-1

Printed in the United States of America

Fifth Edition, 1996

# TABLE OF CONTENTS

| | |
|---|---|
| FORWARD .............................. | v |
| ACKNOWLEDGEMENTS .................. | vii |
| SECTION I   CERTIFICATION GUIDE ....... | 3 |

**SECTION II**
**HUMAN RESOURCE PROFESSIONALISM**

| | |
|---|---|
| Human Resource Professionalism............. | 7 |
| Human Resource Certification Institute ........ | 11 |
| Certification ............................. | 13 |
| Recertification ........................... | 19 |

**SECTION III**
**HR BODY OF KNOWLEDGE**

| | |
|---|---|
| Codification of the Body of Knowledge ......... | 25 |
| HRCI Content Outline ...................... | 29 |
| Resources ............................... | 85 |

**SECTION IV**
**HRCI CERTIFICATION EXAMINATION**

| | |
|---|---|
| Certification Examinations .................. | 95 |
| Examination Preparation Methods, Strategies and Resources .............. | 99 |
| Examination Taking Skills .................. | 113 |
| Practice Examination, Answers, Rationales & Coding ................ | 117 |

**SECTION V**
**FREQUENTLY ASKED QUESTIONS** ........ 221

# FORWARD

The challenge of staying current in the human resource (HR) field demands that individuals in the profession continually update their knowledge and skills. The HR issues of the second half of the 1990s require that HR professionals be able to respond to such widely varying concerns as the changing nature of work and contingent work forces, reengineered work places, virtual offices, boundaryless organizations, employee rights, worker literacy and global competition to name a few.

As the challenges in the field shift, so does the body of knowledge that must be mastered by HR professionals. Consequently, through extensive research conducted by the Human Resource Certification Institute (HRCI), efforts to identify and codify the body of knowledge in HR have been undertaken. From this codification, new and revised content outlines are developed and updated in all HR functional areas. These content outlines form the blueprint for development of the certification examinations offered by HRCI.

The Institute exists to enhance the professionalism of HR practitioners, educators, researchers, and consultants through its certification process. One key part of that process is providing professional certification examinations. Depending upon his/her experience level, an individual in the HR field can attain certification as either a Professional in Human Resources (PHR) or a Senior Professional in Human Resources (SPHR). This guide provides an aid to individuals desirous of becoming certified HR professionals. It is not a preparation tool but instead provides a "road map" to understand the certification process, to assess one's level of preparedness and to focus on areas of needed review.

# ACKNOWLEDGMENTS

This publication would not have been possible without the contribution of the Human Resource Certification Institute Board of Directors, and the many volunteers who help in item and test development. Although too many to recognize individually, their efforts served as a basis for the content of this Certification Guide.

Volunteers are the heart of the Human Resource Certification Institute's program. They are all certified professionals who have successfully passed the Institute's certification examination. They draft test items, review test items, establish passing or cut scores and otherwise support the Institute in its mission.

If volunteers are the heart of the Institute's program, the staff is its soul. Lead by Ed Lyons, SPHR, its Executive Director, the staff consisting of Cornelia Cont, Manager, Program Administration, Kelly Downey, Program Coordinator and Tanya Iberg, Program Assistant are charged with the day-to-day administration of the Institute's program. They serve as a vital link between those currently certified, those wishing to become certified, the Institute's Board and its test vendor. They are the glue that holds the program together. Lastly, much credit goes to the excellent support of Lori Kohn who typed and proofed this manuscript.

# CERTIFICATION

# GUIDE

# CERTIFICATION GUIDE

This Certification Guide was developed with a number of purposes in mind. First, this Guide was designed to provide individuals in the human resource (HR) field relevant information about the Human Resource Certification Institute (HRCI) and its certification process. Second, this Guide describes the Institute's codification process and its result -- a topical outline of the human resource management body of knowledge. Third, this Guide explains various methods of preparing for the Institute's certification examination. Fourth, this Guide provides a practice examination whereby individuals can gauge mastery of the HR body of knowledge.

History has shown two primary reasons why HR practitioners are reluctant to take one of the Institute's certification examinations. First, there is fear of the unknown, such as not knowing what to study or what types of questions will be encountered. Second, and closely related, is the fear of failure -- not knowing one's level of proficiency prior to taking the examination. These two fears, whether real or imagined, prevent many capable human resource practitioners from taking one of the certification examinations. This Guide was designed to help alleviate these two fears.

This publication offers a starting point for formal training or informal self-development for persons interested in individual or group study in the human resource field.

Copies of the Certification Guide may be purchased from SHRM Store, PO Box 930132, Atlanta, GA 31193-0132, 1-800-444-5006. Proceeds from the sales are used to support the Institute's educational purposes and operations. The Certification Program is administered by a headquarters staff to whom inquiries may be addressed:

Human Resource Certification Institute
606 North Washington Street
Alexandria, VA 22314
(703) 548-3440

Fax #(703) 836-0367
TDD # (703) 548-6999
e-mail address: hrci@shrm.org
HRCI homepage: http://www.shrm.org/docs/hrci.html

# HUMAN RESOURCE

# PROFESSIONALISM

# HUMAN RESOURCE PROFESSIONALISM

In the mid 1960's, the American Society for Personnel Administration (now the Society for Human Resource Management), in conjunction with Cornell University, approached the United States Department of Labor with a simple question -- "What constitutes a profession?". The Department of Labor responded that there were five distinct characteristics which separated a profession from other pursuits or endeavors. Those five characteristics as they relate to the human resource field were:

1. <u>National Organization</u> - The first requirement of a profession was a national organization - a national organization that can speak as a unified voice for its members and foster the development of the field. The Society for Human Resource Management (SHRM) fulfills that role for its membership which exceeds 73,000 worldwide.

2. <u>Code of Ethics</u> - The second requirement of a profession was a code of ethics identifying standards of behavior relating to fairness, justice, truthfulness, and social responsibility. SHRM had developed such a code to which all members are expected to adhere.

   Likewise HRCI has developed a Model of Professional Excellence which provides the following ethical standards:

"As certified human resource professionals, our personal standards of honor and integrity must, at all times, be above reproach and we must conduct ourselves in a manner that reflects favorably on our profession.

By adhering to the highest standard of honor and integrity, we as human resource professionals help to create an ethical climate within our organizations.

We have a duty to protect the interests of our employees, the organization and society to promote and encourage the following behaviors:

- Honesty and trustworthiness in all our relationships;
- Reliability in performing our assigned responsibilities;
- Truthfulness and accuracy in what we say and write;
- Constructiveness and cooperation in our working relationships;
- Fairness, consideration, and non-discrimination in how we treat others;
- Adherence to the law in all activities;
- Economical use of resources;
- Commitment to excellence in the performance of our work; and
- Respect for the privacy of others."

3. <u>Research</u> - The third requirement of a profession was the need for applied research to develop the field. The SHRM Foundation each year funds research into new and emerging areas of HR. HRCI provides financial support to the SHRM Foundation in its pursuit of advancing the HR field.

4. <u>Body of Knowledge</u> - The fourth requirement of a profession was a defined body of knowledge. The Institute through its Codification Process defines the HR body of knowledge for practitioners in the field. This body of knowledge is disseminated to professionals through journals and publications some of which are sponsored by SHRM.

5. <u>Credentialing</u> - The last requirement of a profession was a credentialing organization - an organization which sets professional standards in the field. HRCI's eligibility requirements to take its certification examination and successfully passing that examination fulfills this requirement.

SHRM and HRCI together have combined to meet all of the requirements for the human resource field as a profession. Although still a developing profession, the high standards set by these two organizations, plus the high level of performance expected of the human resource function, will make the challenge of professionalism that much greater in the future.

# HUMAN RESOURCE CERTIFICATION INSTITUTE

The Human Resource Certification Institute (HRCI), an affiliate of the Society for Human Resource Management (SHRM), is a non-profit organization whose purpose is to develop and maintain professional standards in the human resource (HR) field. This purpose is accomplished by:

* defining and periodically updating the outline of the body of knowledge of the HR field (Codification Process)

* promoting self-development of individuals in the HR field

* recognizing and credentialing individuals who have met established experience requirements and have demonstrated a mastery of the HR body of knowledge

The first certification examinations were administered in the spring of 1976, following years of extensive work by a task force formed by the American Society for Personnel Administration, forerunner of SHRM. The efforts of this group led to a certification program open to professionals in the HR field.

Today, HRCI is governed by a Board of Directors composed of certified HR individuals, who volunteer their time and effort to advance professionalism in the field. Area Examination Development Directors with the help of volunteer HR experts, are responsible for reviewing the body of knowledge content outlines and bibliographic reference lists and developing test items for the examinations. HRCI employs a highly qualified staff to administer its certification program.

# CERTIFICATION

The Institute offers two levels of certification -- Professional in Human Resources (PHR) and Senior Professional in Human Resources (SPHR). Each level has different experience requirements that must be satisfied before a candidate may take the respective certification examination. The Institute allows for substitution of education in lieu of a portion of the experience requirements. However, there is a minimum experience requirement which must be met no matter how much education a candidate possesses.

In order to take either level of the examination, the following requirements apply.

Eligibility

HRCI grants certification after the applicant has:

1. verified professional exempt-level experience in the HR field (as defined by the Fair Labor Standards Act and its amendments) as either a practitioner, educator, researcher or consultant, and ...

2. passed a comprehensive written examination to demonstrate mastery of the HR Body of Knowledge.

To earn the basic generalist designation
***Professional in Human Resources (PHR)***
one must have
Four years of professional HR Exempt-level experience
OR
Two years HR Exempt-level experience
and a bachelor's degree
OR
One year HR Exempt-level experience
and a graduate degree

AND
Pass a comprehensive examination
****************************************************
To earn a senior generalist designation
***Senior Professional in Human Resources (SPHR)***
one must have
Eight years of professional HR Exempt-level experience
OR
Six years HR Exempt-level experience
and a bachelor's degree
OR
Five years of HR Exempt-level experience
and a graduate degree

AND
Pass a comprehensive examination

Experience must be in the human resource (HR) field in an *Exempt* level position under criteria established by the Fair Labor Standards

Act. Likewise, degrees must be earned from an accredited higher education institution.

Eligibility as a Student or Recent Graduate

HRCI permits and encourages students to sit for the certification exam. To qualify under the *student* category, **a candidate must not be eligible under one of the other categories of eligibility**. Additionally, student candidates are permitted to take the exam no earlier than 12 months prior to their graduation date and recent graduates no later than 12 months after their graduation date. Students/recent graduates have five years from the date of passing the exam to secure their required HR exempt level experience. Upon meeting the experience requirement, students must pay the balance of their certification fee and provide the required employment experience documentation before the PHR certification is awarded. Those candidates qualifying under the student/recent graduate category are **NOT** eligible for SPHR certification.

Definitions

The Human Resource management credentialing program established and administered by the Human Resource Certification Institute is intended for those professionals who are currently working in the field. While that work need not always be exclusively in the HR field, it is expected that work in the field be the dominating thrust. Therefore, the following general definitions apply:

| | |
|---|---|
| PRACTITIONER: | One whose duties are those normally found in the typical HR activity. |
| EDUCATOR: | One whose principal area of instruction is in the HR field in a higher education institution. |

RESEARCHER:          One whose research activities are restricted primarily to the HR field.

CONSULTANT:          One whose consulting activities are predominantly in the HR field.

Use of Certification

The Human Resource Certification Institute Program is voluntary in nature, and such certification is conferred by HRCI solely when a human resource professional has demonstrated achievement of national standards ranging from technical operational knowledge to comprehension of contemporary management concepts and practices. Those persons or organizations who choose to incorporate HRCI certification as a condition of employment or advancement do so of their own volition. Such persons must determine for themselves whether the use of such a certification process, including its eligibility and recertification requirements, when coupled with other requirements imposed by such persons, meets their respective needs and complies with applicable laws.

Applications

The *Certification Information Handbook* is a multi page booklet that provides information about the certification process. It includes an application form to take the examination and summarizes the previously mentioned qualifications. The application packet also contains the current year's examination fee schedule and test center locations. The *Certification Information Handbook* may be obtained by contacting the:

Human Resource Certification Institute
606 North Washington St
Alexandria, VA 22314
(703) 548-3440
FAX: (703) 836-0367
TDD: (703) 548-6999
e-mail: hrci@shrm.org
HRCI homepage: http://www.shrm.org/docs/hrci.html

# RECERTIFICATION

Certification is a well-earned badge of professional ability of one's mastery in a critical and increasingly demanding field. The human resource (HR) field is not static. Rapid change, new dimensions and perspectives require new knowledge and techniques by HR professionals who aim to maintain their professional edge. Hence, **recertification** is a method for certified professionals to demonstrate their accomplishments in keeping abreast of change and updating their knowledge in the HR field.

Recertification is required by HRCI within three years of earning certification and each recertification period is also for three years. There are two methods of recertification, either of which will ensure the retention of the certified designation one has worked so hard to achieve.

**Method One:** Recertification by Examination

All requirements for recertification may be met by passing the current, applicable examination.

**Method Two:** Recertification by the updating of Education and Experience

Recertification through education and experience can be earned by the following career elements in any combination totaling 60 contact hours.

1. <u>Continuing Education:</u> Recertification credit can be earned through attendance at any HR-related courses, workshops, seminars

or conferences. However, the Institute does not accept for recertification credit attendance at regularly held association meetings -such as those which are conducted on a monthly basis. Note: All 60 recertification credit hours may be obtained from this category.

2. <u>Research and/or Publishing:</u> A second way to earn recertification credit is by conducting an HR related research project or by writing and publishing in the HR field - however, the authoring of an article published in a "Newsletter" will not meet this requirement. Note: one may earn up to a total of 20 hours of the required 60 from this category.

3. <u>Instruction:</u> Another recertification credit-earning activity is preparation for and the teaching of a new college-level class or presentation at a workshop or conference (including in-house training programs). Note: one may be credited with up to 20 hours of the required 60 from this category only for the first time the presentation is made.

4. <u>One-The-Job:</u> Certain projects at work may earn recertification credit. A first-time work activity that adds to the certified professional's HR knowledge base may be counted as credit. The focus in this area is upon capturing <u>new</u> knowledge. Note: No more than 10 of the required 60 hours of recertification credit may be earned by this method.

5. <u>Leadership:</u> Leadership experience may also earn recertification credit for the certified professional. Up to 10 credit hours may be earned through leadership responsibilities in an HR professional organization such as SHRM at national, area, state or local levels or in a civic/community activity where one's HR knowledge is the primary reason for the affiliation.

6.   <u>Professional Membership:</u>  Recertification credit is available for professionals who maintain national membership in professional societies/associations. A maximum of 10 credit hours may be earned through professional membership. Note: Credit hours are available only if national SHRM membership is maintained.

<u>Recertification Application and Fees</u>

Application forms, both for recertification by examination and for recertification by documentation, are available from the Institute. Each form contains the current fee for recertification and the steps necessary under that method to apply.

# HUMAN RESOURCE BODY OF KNOWLEDGE

# CODIFICATION OF THE BODY OF KNOWLEDGE

What should a human resource practitioner know and be able to apply in order to be considered a competent HR generalist? This is a fundamental question HRCI seeks to answer through its Codification Process. The Codification Process is an extensive ongoing research program designed to specifically define the HR body of knowledge.

The HR field is dynamic and in a constant state of change. The knowledge requirements for practice must reflect this ever present change. HRCI's Codification Process attempts to keep HR knowledge requirements both relevant and up-to-date.

In order to set standards for the credentialing of a profession, the relevant body of knowledge must first be specifically defined. The body of knowledge serves as the foundation upon which HRCI's entire certification program is built. From this body of knowledge, a content outline is developed. In turn, this content outline serves as a blueprint for the certification examination construction. Examination items are developed to measure the knowledge requirements which reflect the topics on the content outline.

The end result of this research is a set of assurances. Assurances that HRCI certification:

- is based on a set of well-defined knowledge requirements,

- is current and able to respond to rapid changes in the field of practice,

- is based upon "real life" human resource management, and

- is focused on important knowledge and not trivial matters.

Codification research began in 1976 with a group of HR content area experts from throughout the nation. Their role was to critique draft content outlines and weightings, recommend revisions, suggest sources for the bibliographies, and make other pertinent comments.

In 1979 and again in 1984, a modified Delphi technique involving hundreds of professionals was used to revise the content outlines. This method used a multiple nomination technique to identify experts who were widely known and respected as HR leaders.

The experts included practitioners, educators, researchers, and consultants. They were asked to perform a highly detailed evaluation of the content outlines and bibliographies. Statistical analyses were performed, and the resulting body of knowledge represented the consensus views of those experts.

Prior to 1988, the methodology used in the codification process involved using human resource experts for a normative (or what the field ought to be) perspective. In 1988, the Personnel Accreditation Institute, with funding supplied by the ASPA Foundation, went to the "real" experts in the HR field for a descriptive (the way it is) perspective. A detailed survey questionnaire consisting of 234 separate items was mailed to over 41,000 human resource practitioners, educators, researchers and consultants. Participants were asked to evaluate each of the questions in terms of how essential it was to their particular job. In addition, a number of demographic factors were solicited to allow for more in-depth analyses of data.

The data from the codification questionnaire was reviewed by the HRCI Board in conjunction with the respective SHRM National Committee Chairs. That data was then compiled into a comprehensive content outline which serves as the foundation of the current HRCI content outline.

In order to verify and revise the HRCI content outline between major surveys of practitioners, HRCI uses expert reviews, an extensive literature search and an analysis of HR textbooks. This form of "environmental scan" identifies new knowledge requirements and those which may be obsolete. A major environmental scan took place in 1992. The resulting revisions to the content outline represents a blending of the descriptive and normative perspectives that provide a comprehensive definition of the HR body of knowledge as contained in this *Certification Guide*.

This codified body of knowledge is used as a basis for certification testing and for the preparation of these publications/products:

- HRCI Certification Information Handbook

- HRCI Certification Guide

- HRCI College and University Curriculum Guide

- SHRM Learning System

- SHRM Certification Preparation Course

The HR body of knowledge is much like a moving target. Consequently, the Institute's research in this area is continuing in order to ensure that the content outlines and certification examination always reflect current HR knowledge and practice.

# HRCI CONTENT OUTLINE

The HRCI content outline is divided into six functional areas. The weighting of each area is based on its relative importance to the knowledge requirements of an HR generalist. The PHR and SPHR examinations are weighted accordingly:

|  | PHR | SPHR |
|---|---|---|
| Management Practices | 22% | 29% |
| Selection and Placement | 20 | 15 |
| Training and Development | 12 | 12 |
| Compensation and Benefits | 21 | 18 |
| Employee and Labor Relations | 18 | 19 |
| Health, Safety, and Security | 7 | 7 |
|  | 100% | 100% |

The numbers in parentheses indicate the percentage composition for each major functional area and sub-area. The first number is the PHR percentage and the second number is the SPHR percentage.

I. **Management Practices (22%, 29%)**

    A. Role of HR in Organizations (3.15, 3.99%)

        1. HR Roles: Advisory Role, Service Role, Control Role
        2. Change Agent Role

        3. HR's Role in Strategic Planning

        4. HR Generalist and HR Specialist Roles

        5. Effects of Different Organizational Contexts and Industries on HR Functions

        6. HR Policies and Procedures

            a. Formation and administration of policies and procedures
            b. Policy manuals and employee handbooks
            c. Employee communications: newsletters, bulletins, memos

        7. Integration and Coordination of HR Functions

    B. Human Resource Planning (3.01%, 3.99%)

        1. Environmental Scanning

       a. Economic conditions
       b. Competition
       c. Technological advances
       d. Labor force trends
       e. Geographic and demographic considerations
       f. Government and regulatory agencies

2. Forecast of Internal HR Supply and Demand

       a. Business strategy
       b. Anticipated skill/labor needs
       c. Trend and ratio analysis and projections
       d. Turnover analysis

3. Inventory of Human Resources

       a. Knowledge, abilities, skills, and experience of present employees
       b. Replacement charts, succession planning

4. Human Resource Information Systems

       a. HRIS functions and uses
       b. System implementation: PC or mainframe
       c. Evaluation of needs

d. Alternatives and criteria in selecting a system
   e. Cost/savings analysis

5. Action Plans and Programs

   a. Career pathing
   b. Training
   c. Transfers
   d. Promotions
   e. Recruitment
   f. Attrition
   g. Early retirement
   h. Employee leasing

6. Evaluation of Human Resource Planning

C. Organizational Design and Development (2.12%, 3.20%)

1. Organizational Structures

   a. Functional vs. product departmentalization
   b. Centralized vs. decentralized decision making
   c. Formal vs. informal rules and control mechanisms
   d. Specialized vs. enlarged task assignments

                e.   Span of control
                f.   Matrix structures
                g.   Reengineering
                h.   Linkage of organizational structure to HR plans: line vs. staff
                I.   Evaluation of structure/design effectiveness

        2.   Organizational Development

                a.   Organizational change: change theories, anticipating and facilitating change
                b.   Organizational development approaches: interpersonal, technological, structural
                c.   Diagnosis and intervention strategies: action research, sensing, team building, goal setting, survey feedback, strategic planning, visioning, sensitivity training (T-groups), grid training
                d.   Role of organizational culture in organizational development

D.   Budgeting, Controlling, and Measurement (1.30%, 1.75%)

        1.   HR Budgeting Process

                a.      Linking to financial plans
                b.      Costing HR programs

      2.     HR Control Process

              a.      Policies
              b.      Procedures
              c.      Rules

      3.     Evaluating HR Effectiveness

              a.      HR measures
              b.      HR audit

E.    Motivation (1.71%, 2.08%)

      1.     Motivation Theories

              a.      Expectancy theory
              b.      Equity theory
              c.      Self theories: self-esteem, self-actualization, self-efficiency
              d.      Learning and reinforcement theories
              e.      Need theories

      2.     Applying Motivation Theory in Management

              a.      Motivation and compensation/financial incentives

       b. Motivation and goal setting
       c. Motivation and job satisfaction
       d. Motivation and productivity
       e. Cross-cultural differences

F. Leadership (1.83%, 2.32%)

    1. Leadership Theories

       a. Leader traits: skills, abilities, qualities, and traits of good leaders
       b. Leader behaviors: concern for people, concern for the task
       c. Situational or contingency leadership theories

    2. Effect of Leadership in Organizations

       a. Transformational vs. transactional leaders
       b. Styles of leadership
       c. Gender differences
       d. Cross-cultural differences

    3. Leadership Training

    4. Roles in Leadership: Leader's Role, Follower's Role

G. Quality and Performance Management/TQM (2.20%, 2.81%)

    1. Performance Planning: Identifying Goals/Desired Behaviors

    2. Setting and Communicating Performance Standards

    3. Measuring Results and Providing Feedback

    4. Implementing Performance Improvement Strategies

    5. Evaluating Results

H. Employee Involvement Strategies (2.35%, 2.80%)

    1. Work Teams

        a. Self-directed work teams
        b. Quality circles
        c. Task forces

    2. Job Design and Redesign

    3. Employee Ownership/ESOP's

    4. Employee Suggestion System

5. Participative Management

   a. Manager's role in participative management
   b. Labor union's role in participative management
   c. Legal issues in participative management
   d. When participative management is appropriate vs. inappropriate

6. Alternative Work Schedules

   a. Flextime
   b. Compressed work weeks
   c. Regular or "permanent" part-time
   d. Job sharing
   e. Phased retirement
   f. Home-based work or telecommuting

7. Role of HR in Employee Involvement Programs

I. HR Research (1.16%, 1.73%)

  1. Research Design and Methodology

     a. Scientific method
     b. Experimental design

                c.      Data-gathering methods

      2.      Quantitative Analysis

                a.      Reliability and validity
                b.      Statistics: descriptive, inferential
                c.      Correlation and regression

      3.      Qualitative Research

J.      International HR Management (1.40%, 2.25%)

      1.      Cultural Differences

                a.      Cross-country comparisons
                b.      Managerial styles

      2.      Legal Aspects of International HR

                a.      Workers' rights
                b.      Legal differences between countries
                c.      Different tax laws
                d.      Immigration laws

      3.      Expatriation and Repatriation

                a.      Selection of expatriates
                b.      Training and preparation of expatriates

- c. Adjustment of expatriate's spouse and family
- d. Failures and problems of expatriates
- e. Retention of expatriates
- f. Challenges and problems of repatriation

4. Issues of Multinational Corporations

   - a. Local vs. expatriate managers
   - b. Communication and language problems
   - c. Societal and environmental impact on local country

5. Compensation and Benefits for Foreign Nationals and Expatriates

   - a. Cost of living allowances
   - b. Exchange rate fluctuations
   - c. Inflation rates

6. The Role of HR in International Business

   - a. International HR trends
   - b. Role of HR in international joint ventures, mergers, acquisitions, etc.

K. Ethics (1.78%, 2.08%)

    1. Ethical Issues

        a. Privacy in the workplace: electronic surveillance, confidentiality of personnel files, employee testing/performance appraisals
        b. Conflicts of interest
        c. Bribes, payoffs, and kickbacks
        d. Whistle blowing
        e. Deceptive practices
        f. Forms of organizational abuse: unintentional injury to employees

    2. Establishing Ethical Behavior in the Organization

        a. Organizational code of ethics
        b. Ethics training programs
        c. Practices, policies, and systems to support and encouraging ethical behavior (reward systems, selection process, etc.)

## II. Selection and Placement (20%, 15%)

A. Legal and Regulatory Factors Affecting Selection and Placement: Definitions, Requirements, Proscribed Practices,

Exemptions, Enforcement, Remedies, and
Case Histories (6.11%, 4.39%)

1. Title VII of the Civil Rights Act (1964) as amended (1972, 1991)

2. Executive Order 11246 (1965) as amended by 11375 (1967), and Executive Order 11478 (1969)

3. Age Discrimination in Employment Act (1967) as amended

4. Consumer Credit Protection Act: Fair Credit Reporting (1970)

5. Vocational Rehabilitation Act (1973) as amended

6. Vietnam-era Veterans Readjustment Act (1974)

7. Pregnancy Discrimination in Employment Act (1978)

8. Immigration Reform and Control Act (1986) as amended (1990)

9. Employee Polygraph Protection Act (1988)

10. Uniform Guidelines on Employee Selection Procedures

11. Worker Adjustment and Retraining Notification Act (1988)

12. Americans with Disabilities Act (1990)

13. Common Law Tort Theories

    a. Employment-at-will
    b. Negligent hiring
    c. Defamation
    d. Invasion of privacy
    e. Constructive discharge

B. Equal Employment Opportunity/Affirmative Action (2.61%, 2.11%)

    1. Legal Endorsement of EEO: Supreme Court Decisions

    2. Equal Employment Opportunity Programs

        a. Work-force analysis
        b. Record-keeping and reporting requirements
        c. Applicant flow
        d. Adverse impact analysis: 4/5ths rule
        e. Impact of changing demographics

3. Affirmative Action Plans

   a. Policy development
   b. Work force analysis
   c. Availability analysis
   d. Under-utilization/concentration
   e. Goals and timetables
   f. Supportive in-house programs
   g. Auditing
   h. Consequences of non-compliance

4. Special Programs to Eliminate Discrimination

   a. Managing/valuing diversity
   b. Sensitivity and awareness training
   c. Reasonable accommodations for the disabled

5. Fairness Issues: Reverse Discrimination, Quota Hiring vs. Merit Hiring

C. Recruitment (3.07%, 2.29%)

   1. Determining Recruitment Needs and Objectives
      a. Needs analysis
      b. Cost of recruiting
      c. Selection ratio

2. Identifying Selection Criteria

   a. Job analysis
   b. Job description
   c. Job qualifications

3. Internal Sourcing

   a. Job posting and bidding
   b. Current and former employees
   c. Skill banks, skill tracking systems

4. External Sourcing

   a. Employee referrals
   b. Educational institutions/college recruiting
   c. Labor unions
   d. Trade and competitive sources
   e. Third-party sources: public and private employment agencies, search firms, temporary help agencies, executive recruiters (head-hunters)
   f. Media: newspapers, trade journals, professional journals, radio, television
   g. Employee data bases
   h. Career/job fairs

5. Evaluating Recruiting Effectiveness

   a. Internal vs. external
   b. Short range vs. long range
   c. Effectiveness/efficiency measures: cost-per-hire, fill time, turnover, yield ratios

D. Selection (6.47%, 4.69%)

   1. Application Process

      a. Applicant flow
      b. Application forms
      c. Weighted application blanks
      d. Applicant notification
      e. Legal/privacy issues

   2. Interviewing

      a. Interviewing skills and techniques
      b. Legality of questions
      c. Types of interviews: patterned, structured, behavioral, non-directive, stress, board
      d. Interpretation of body language/non-verbal behavior
      e. Interviewer impressions/biases
      f. Team/group interviews
      g. Reliability and validity

3. Pre-employment Testing

   a. Intelligence/aptitude/skills testing
   b. Motor and physical abilities
   c. Psychological/personality profiles
   d. Honesty/integrity testing
   e. Assessment center
   f. Legal/privacy issues
   g. Polygraph
   h. Reliability and validity

4. Background Investigation

   a. References: academic, work, financial, personal, credit, etc.
   b. Legal questions
   c. Privacy/defamation issues
   c. Negligent hiring

5. Medical Examination

   a. Physical examination
   b. Drug testing
   c. ADA restrictions and reasonable accommodations
   d. Legal/privacy issues

6. Hiring Disabled Applicants

   a. Definition of a disabled person

             b.    Discriminatory practice under the ADA
             c.    Acceptable pre-employment inquiries under ADA
             d.    Reasonable accommodations

      7.    Illegal Use of Drugs and Alcohol

      8.    Validation and Evaluation of Selection Process Components

             a.    Cost/benefit analysis
             b.    Reliability
             c.    Content validity
             d.    Construct validity
             e.    Criterion-related validity

E.    Career Planning and Development (1.73%, 1.53%)

      1.    Accommodating Organizational and Individual Needs

             a.    Integrating career development and HR planning
             b.    Career strategies
             c.    Career counseling
             d.    Career pathing
             e.    Dual careers
             f.    Mommy track/daddy track

2. Mobility Within the Organization

    a. Promotions
    b. Demotions
    c. Relocations
    d. Transfers

3. Managing Transitions

    a. Misplacement and displacement
    b. Outplacement
    c. Early retirement
    d. Job search strategies
    e. Retraining
    f. Mergers
    g. Acquisitions
    h. Restructuring
    i. Integration
    j. Downsizing

## III. Training and Development (12%, 12%)

A. Legal and Regulatory Factors Affecting Training: Definitions, Requirements, Proscribed Practices, Exemptions, Enforcement, Remedies and Case Histories (2.03%, 1.94%)

1. Title VII of the Civil Rights Act (1964, 1991), Americans with Disabilities Act

(1990), and other applicable employment discrimination statutes

    2.    National Labor Relations Act (1935), Labor-Management Relations Act (1947), and other applicable labor relations statutes

    3.    Copyright Statutes

    4.    OSHA Mandated Training

B.    HR Training and the Organization (1.65%, 1.98%)

    1.    Linking Training to Organizational Goals, Objectives, and Strategies

    2.    Funding the Training Function

    3.    Cost/Benefit Analysis of Training

C.    Training Needs Analysis (.93%, .94%)

    1.    Training Needs Analysis Process

        a.    Objectives of needs analysis
        b.    Types of needs analysis: organizational, task, and individual

2. Methods for Assessing Training Needs

    a. Surveys/questionnaires
    b. Interviews
    c. Performance data (results and appraisals)
    d. Anticipated future skill needs
    e. Anticipated changes in labor pool
    f. Observations/audits
    g. Tests
    h. Assessment centers
    i. Focus groups/group discussions
    j. Document reviews
    k. Advisory committees

D. Training and Development Programs (5.17%, 4.92%)

1. Trainer Selection

    a. Internal training department
    b. External consultants
    c. Public training programs/seminars

2. Design Considerations and Learning Principles

    a. Determining training objectives
    b. Principles and models of learning
    c. Selection of participants and trainers

        d.      Evaluating learning readiness
        e.      Selecting learning strategies
        f.      Training methods and processes

3. Types of Training Programs

        a.      Skill development: sales/customer-based, technical, computer-based, JIT: job instruction training
        b.      Attitude and information: sexual harassment prevention, ethics, AIDS awareness, quality, diversity
        c.      Management and supervisor: executive development, supervisory and managerial development
        d.      General and personal development: creativity, literacy, writing skills, career planning
        e.      Orientation

4. Instructional Methods and Processes

        a.      Coaching/mentoring
        b.      Rotation/cross training
        c.      Internships/apprenticeships
        d.      Role playing/simulation
        e.      Workshops/seminars
        f.      Computer-assisted/programmed instruction
        g.      Vestibule/laboratory

                h.   On-the-job vs. off-the job
                i.   Correspondence
                j.   Teletraining
                k.   Assessment centers

        5.  Training Facilities Planing

                a.   On-site/off-site
                b.   Space requirements
                c.   Seating arrangements
                d.   Environmental considerations
                e.   Accessibility (ADA)

        6.  Training Materials

                a.   Manuals
                b.   Handouts
                c.   Leader guides
                d.   Audio-visual materials

E.  Evaluation of Training Effectiveness (2.23%, 2.22%)

        1.  Sources for Evaluation

                a.   Questionnaires and surveys
                b.   Performance tests
                c.   Interviews
                d.   Simulations
                e.   Ratings/checklists
                f.   Critical incidents

g. Observations
h. Performance appraisals

2. Research Methods for Evaluation

   a. Experimental designs and use of control groups
   b. Quasi-experimental designs

3. Criteria for Evaluating Training

   a. Reactions of participants
   b. Learning new skills/competencies
   c. Behavioral changes
   d. Measurable results

## IV. Compensation and Benefits (21%, 18%)

A. Legal and Regulatory Factors Affecting Compensation and Benefits: Definitions, Requirements, Proscribed Practices, Exemptions, Enforcement, Remedies, and Case Histories (4.14%, 3.03%)

1. Early Compensation Laws: Davis-Bacon Act (1931); Anti-kickback (Copland) Act (1934); Public Contracts (Walsh-Healy) Act (1936)

2. Fair Labor Standards Act (1938) as amended

        a. Exempt vs. nonexempt
        b. Overtime provisions and computations; regular workweek, regular rate, compensatory time, fluctuating workweeks
        c. Minimum wages
        d. Child labor
        e. Record keeping

3. Equal Pay Act (1963)

        a. Equal pay for equal work
        b. Permissible wage differentials

4. Title VII of the Civil Rights Act (1964) as amended (1972, 1991)

5. Age Discrimination in Employment Act (1967) as amended

6. Consumer Credit Protection Act: Wage Garnishment (1968), Fair Credit Reporting (1970)

7. HMO (Health Maintenance Organization Act) (1973)

8. ERISA (Employee Retirement Income Security Act) (1974)

9. Pregnancy Discrimination in Employment Act (1978)

10. COBRA (Consolidated Omnibus Budget Reconciliation Act) (1985)

11. Workers' Compensation and Unemployment Compensation Laws/Regulations

12. Social Security Laws and Regulations

13. Family and Medical Leave Act (1993)

B. Tax and Accounting Treatment of Compensation and Benefit Programs (.50%,.52%)

1. FASB Regulations

2. IRS Regulations

C. Economic Factors Affecting Compensation (1.01%, 0.99%)

1. Inflation

2. Interest Rates

3. Foreign Competition

4. Economic Growth

D. Total Compensation Philosophy, Strategy, and Policy (1.61%, 1.51%)

    1. Fitting Strategy and Policy to the External Environment and to the Organization's Culture, Structure, and Objectives

    2. Training and Communication of Compensation Programs

    3. Making Compensation Programs Achieve Organizational Objectives

        a. Internally and externally equitable
        b. Motivating
        c. Provides a secure and adequate income
        d. Cost/benefit effective for the organization

    4. Establishing Administrative Controls

        a. Compensation/benefits budgets
        b. Policies and procedures
        c. Performance measures

E. Compensation Programs: Types, Characteristics, and Advantages/Disadvantages (2.03%, 1.72%)

1. Base Pay

    a.  Time-based
    b.  Performance-based
    c.  Productivity-based
    d.  Skill/knowledge based

2. Differential Pay

    a.  Overtime
    b.  Shift pay
    c.  Hazard pay
    d.  On-call pay
    e.  Call-back pay
    f.  Geographic differentials

3. Incentive Pay

    a.  Individual
    b.  Groups and teams: gainsharing, improshare
    c.  Organization-wide programs: scanlon plans, profit sharing
    d.  Short and long term
    e.  Cash and stock-based programs

4. Pay Programs for Selected Employees

    a.  Executives
    b.  Direct sales personnel

          c.     Professionals
          d.     Outside directors
          e.     International employees: expatriates, foreign nationals

F.     Job Analysis, Job Description, and Job Specification (1.63%, 1.14%)

     1.     Methods of Job Analysis

          a.     Observations
          b.     Interviews
          c.     Questionnaires
          d.     Functional job analysis
          e.     Records

     2.     Types of Data Gathered in a Job Analysis

          a.     Tasks
          b.     Performance standards
          c.     Responsibilities/Essential Job Functions
          d.     Knowledge required
          e.     Skills required
          f.     Experience needed

        g.     Job content
        h.     Duties
        i.     Equipment used

3. Uses of Job Analysis

        a.     Formulating job descriptions/specifications
        b.     Designing jobs
        c.     Recruiting
        d.     Selection and placement
        e.     New-employee orientation
        f.     Training and development
        g.     Performance appraisal
        h.     Compensation

4. Job Descriptions

        a.     DOT (Dictionary of Occupational titles)
        b.     Job title and location
        c.     Tasks, duties, responsibilities
        d.     Organizational relationships
        e.     Relation to other jobs
        f.     Machines, tools, and materials
        g.     Working conditions

5. Job Specifications

        a.     Education necessary

           b.      Required experience
           c.      Training/skills requirements
           d.      Physical demands

      6.     Validity and Reliability of Job Analysis, Job Description, and Job Specification

G.    Job Evaluation Methods (1.75%, 1.45%)

      1.     Compensable Factors

      2.     Ranking Method

      3.     Classification/Grading Method

      4.     Factor Comparison Method

      5.     Point Method

      6.     Guide Chart-Profile Method (Hay method)

H.    Job Pricing, Pay Structures, and Pay Rate Administration (1.67%, 1.30%)

      1.     Job Pricing and Pay Structures

           a.      Pay ranges
           b.      Pay grades
           c.      Comparable worth
           d.      Red-circle job rates

e. Adjustments for inflation

2. Individual Pay Rate Determination

    a. Performance
    b. Experience
    c. Seniority
    d. Potential

3. Utilizing Performance Appraisal in Pay Administration

4. Reflecting Geographic Influences in Pay Structures

5. Wage Surveys

    a. Government surveys
    b. Private industry surveys
    c. Organization-sponsored surveys

I. Employee Benefit Programs: Types, Objectives, Characteristics, and Advantages/Disadvantages (2.58%, 1.91%)

1. Legally Required Programs/Payments

    a. Social Security
    b. Workers' compensation
    c. Unemployment compensation

2. Income Replacement

   a. Disability
   b. Death
   c. Retirement

3. Insurance and Income Protection

   a. Medical
   b. Dental
   c. Child care
   d. Legal assistance
   e. Elder care
   f. Vision
   g. Auto and property
   h. Unemployment
   i. Severance pay

4. Deferred Pay

   a. Savings
   b. Profit sharing
   c. Deferred salary
   d. Deferred incentives
   e. Stock ownership

5. Pay for Time Not Worked

   a. Vacations
   b. Holidays

        c.    Sick pay
        d.    Paid leave
        e.    Community service
        f.    Sabbaticals
        g.    Bereavement

6. Unpaid Leave

        a.    Jury duty
        b.    Military leave
        c.    Family/medical leave
        d.    Continuation of benefits during unpaid leave

7. Flexible Benefit Plans, Cafeteria Plans

8. Recognition and Achievement Awards
        a.    Performance
        b.    Length of service

J. Managing Employee Benefit Programs (2.87%, 3.09%)

1. Employee Benefits Philosophy, Planning, and Strategy

2. Employee Need/Preference Assessment: Surveys

3. Administrative Systems

4. Funding/Investment Responsibilities

5. Coordination with Plan Trustees, Insurers, Health Service Providers and Third-Party Administrators

6. Utilization Review

7. Cost-Benefit Analysis and Cost Management

8. Communicating Benefit Programs

K. Evaluating the Effectiveness of Total Compensation Strategy and Programs (1.21%, 1.34%)

1. Budgeting

2. Cost Management

3. Assessment of Methods and Processes

V. **Employee and Labor Relations (18%, 19%)**

A. Legal and Regulatory Factors Affecting Employee and Labor Relations: Definitions, Requirements, Proscribed Practices, Exemptions, Enforcement, Remedies, and Case Histories (2.61%, 2.51%)

1. Federal Anti-Injunction (Norris-LaGuardia) Act (1932)

2. National Labor Relations (Wagner) Act (1935)

3. Labor Management Relations (Taft-Hartley) Act (1947)

4. Labor Management Reporting and Disclosure (Landrum-Griffin) Act (1959)

5. Title VII of the Civil Rights Act (1964) as amended (1991) and other applicable employment discrimination statues

6. Age Discrimination in Employment Act (1967) as amended

7. Employee Polygraph Protection Act (1988)

8. Worker Adjustment and Retraining Notification (Plant Closing) Act (1988)

9. Americans with Disabilities Act (1990)

B. Union Representation of Employees (1.40%, 1.54%)

1. Scope of the Labor Management Relations (Taft-Hartley) Act

   a. Commerce requirement
   b. Excluded employees

2. Achieving Representative Status

   a. Demand for recognition
   b. Voluntary recognition
   c. Polling of employees

3. Petitioning for an NLRB Election

   a. Filing and review of a petition
   b. Selecting the bargaining unit
   c. Bars to an election petition
   d. Decertification
   e. Deauthorization and unit clarification petitions

4. Election Campaign

   a. Type: consent or directed
   b. Voter eligibility: full-time, part-time, temporary, seasonal, probationary employees
   c. Time and place
   d. Post-election proceedings: challenges and objections

5. Union Security

   a. Closed shop vs open shop
   b. Union shop
   c. Agency shop

d. Maintenance of membership
e. Dues check-off

C. Employer Unfair Labor Practices (1.54%, 1.64%)

1. Procedures for Processing Unfair Labor Practice

   a. Filing a charge with the NLRB: who, where, how, when, what
   b. Preliminary NLRB investigation and settlement agreements: formal and informal
   c. Complaints and hearings
   d. Judicial review of NLRB orders

2. Interference, Restraint, and Coercion

   a. Unlawful acts of supervisors
   b. Threats of reprisals
   c. Promises and grants of benefits
   d. Solicitation of grievances
   e. Restricting employee activity
   f. Surveillance and interrogation of employees
   g. Inciting antiunion activity
   h. Discrimination for exercising rights
   i. Discipline/discharge for union activity
   j. No-solicitation rules

3. Domination and Unlawful Support of Labor Organizations

    a. Financial assistance
    b. Use of company facilities
    c. Employee participation committees

4. Employee Discrimination to Discourage Union Membership

5. Retaliation

6. Remedies

    a. Bargaining orders
    b. Reinstatement
    c. Cease and desist orders

D. Union Unfair Labor Practices, Strikes, and Boycotts (1.39%, 1.66%)

1. Responsibility for Acts of Union Agents

2. Union Restraint or Coercion

3. Duty of Fair Representation

    a. Good faith
    b. Discrimination and internal union affairs

4. Inducing Unlawful Discrimination by Employer

5. Excessive or Discriminatory Membership Fees

6. Strikes and Secondary Boycotts

    a. Economic strike vs. unfair labor practice strike
    b. Protected and unprotected activity
    c. Replacement of strikers
    d. Compensation during strike
    e. Sympathy and safety strikes
    f. Scope of secondary boycott prohibition
    g. Ally doctrine
    h. Single employer
    i. Common situs picketing
    j. Separate or "reserve gate" doctrine
    k. Consumer picketing
    l. Unlawful picketing
    m. Wildcat strikes, sitdown strikes
    n. "Hot cargo" clauses
    o. Recognitional/organizational picketing

7. Strike Preparation

    a. Pre-strike/during

b. Moving personnel in and out of facility

E. Collective Bargaining (2.37%, 2.91%)

1. Bargaining Issues and Concepts

   a. Illegal items
   b. Mandatory items
   c. Voluntary items
   d. Management prerogatives
   e. Duty to bargain
   f. Parallel bargaining
   g. Coalition and coordinated bargaining

2. Negotiation Strategies

   a. Opening demands
   b. Distributive vs. integrative bargaining
   c. Costing the demands
   d. Bargaining zones
   e. Negotiation tactics

3. Good Faith Requirements

   a. Duty to provide relevant information
   b. Employer defense to duty to disclose: union bad faith
   c. Confidentiality
   d. Waiver

            e.      Unlawful circumvention

    4.     Notice Requirements

    5.     Unilateral Changes in Terms of Employment

    6.     Duty to Successor Employers of Unions:
           Buyouts, Mergers, or Bankruptcy

    7.     Enforcement Provisions

            a.      Grievance and arbitration procedures
            b.      Roles of courts
            c.      Suits by employers and individual
                    employees
            d.      NLRB enforcement

    8.     Injunctions

    9.     Mediation and Conciliation

    10.    National Emergency Strikes

F.  Managing Organization-Union Relations
    (1.04%, 1.18%)

    1.     Building and Maintaining Union-
           Organization Relationships: Cooperative
           Programs

2. Grievance Processes and Procedures

    a. Grievable items
    b. Steps in process
    c. Preparation for grievance

3. Arbitration Process

    a. Preparing for arbitration
    b. Selecting an arbitrator
    c. Items for arbitration
    d. Compulsory arbitration
    e. Binding arbitration

4. Maintaining Nonunion Status

G. Public Sector Labor Relations (0.70%, 0.79%)

1. Right to Organize

2. Federal Labor Relations Council

3. Limitations on Strikes

4. Mediation and Conciliation

H. Employment Policies and Practices (1.61%, 1.40%)

    1. Discipline

        a. Rules and regulations
        b. Kinds of disciplinary problems
        c. Progressive discipline
        d. Administrative justice: due process, just cause

    2. Absenteeism and Tardiness

        a. Causes
        b. Measurement
        c. Remedies

    3. Sexual Harassment

        a. Policies
        b. Investigation
        c. Discipline

    4. Terminations

        a. General
        b. Layoffs
        c. Constructive discharge
        d. Retaliatory
        e. Retirement

I. Individual Employment Rights (1.10%, 1.12%)

    1. Common Law Tort Theories

        a. Defamation
        b. Invasion of privacy
        c. Negligence
        d. Intentional infliction of emotional stress
        e. Fraudulent misrepresentation

    2. Job-As-Property Doctrine

        a. Due process in termination
        b. Just cause actions

    3. Employment-At-Will Doctrine

        a. Violations of public policy
        b. Implied contract
        c. Implied covenant

    4. Exceptions to Employment-At-Will

J. Performance Appraisals (3.16%, 3.13%)

    1. Performance Measurement - The Criterion

        a. Composite
        b. Multiple

       c.      Relevance

2.      Criterion Problems

       a.      Deficiency
       b.      Contamination
       c.      Biases

3.      Documenting Employee Performance

4.      Category Rating Appraisal Methods

       a.      Graphic rating scales
       b.      Forced choice
       c.      Checklists

5.      Comparative Appraisal Methods

       a.      Forced distribution
       b.      Ranking
       c.      Paired comparison

6.      Narrative Appraisal Methods

       a.      Essays
       b.      Critical incidents
       c.      Field review

7. Special Appraisal Methods: MBO, BARS, BOS

   a. Management by objectives
   b. Behavioral anchored rating scales
   c. Behavioral observation scales

8. Types of Appraisals

   a. Supervisor appraisals
   b. Peer appraisals
   c. Subordinate appraisals

9. Rating Errors

   a. Halo/horn effect
   b. Recency
   c. Bias
   d. Strictness
   e. Leniency
   f. Central tendency
   g. Contrast

10. Appraisal Interview

    a. Environment
    b. Methods
    c. Styles

11. Linking Appraisals to Selection, Compensation, and Training and Development

12. Legal Constraints on Performance Appraisal

K. Employee Attitudes, Opinions, and Satisfaction (1.08%, 1.13%)

1. Measurement

   a. Exit interviews
   b. Survey design
   c. Survey administration
   d. Results analysis
   e. Interpretation

2. Feedback
   a. Feedback to management
   b. Feedback to employees

3. Intervention

   a. Plans for change
   b. Implementation of plans
   c. Follow-up
   d. Evaluation

4. Confidentiality and Anonymity of Surveys

## VI. Health, Safety, and Security (7%, 7%)

    A.    Legal and Regulatory Factors Affecting Health, Safety and Security: Definitions, Requirements, Proscribed Practices, Exemptions, Enforcement, Remedies, and Case Histories (1.42%, 1.32%)

        1.    Occupational Safety and Health Act (1970)

            a.    Enforcement standards
            b.    Worker rights
            c.    Recordkeeping
            d.    Inspection requirements
            e.    Citations and violations
            f.    Criminal penalties

        2.    Vocational Rehabilitation Act (1973) as amended

            a.    Definition of handicap
            b.    Requirements of federal contractors
            c.    Application to AIDS, tuberculosis, etc.

        3.    Drug-Free Workplace Act (1988)

            a.    Drug-free workplace policies and programs
            b.    Required action in drug-related convictions

4. Hazard Communication Standards (1986)

5. Americans with Disabilities Act (1990)

B. Health (2.66%, 2.58%)

    1. Analysis of Environmental factors

        a. Epidemiology
        b. Environmental toxicology

    2. Employee Assistance Programs

        a. Employee counseling
        b. Administration
        c. In-house vs. contract
        d. Referral process
        e. Confidentiality
        f. Measuring cost and personal effectiveness

    3. Employee Wellness Programs

        a. Types of programs: weight reduction, smoking cessation, fitness, stress reduction, etc.
        b. Promoting wellness programs
        c. Measuring cost effectiveness

4. Fetal Protection Policies

5. Chemical Dependency

   a. Identification of symptoms
   b. Drug testing
   c. Referral processes
   d. Discipline
   e. Supervisory training
   f. Employee awareness

6. Communicable Diseases in the Workplace

   a. AIDS
   b. Tuberculosis
   c. Hepatitis
   d. OSHA Blood-Borne Pathogen Standard

7. Employer Liabilities

   a. Toxic substances
   b. Radiation

8. Stress Management

   a. Burnout
   b. Sources of stress
   c. Coping strategies

9. Smoking Policies

10. Recordkeeping and Reporting

C. Safety (1.78%, 1.74%)

    1. Organization of Safety Program

        a. Management support
        b. Roles and responsibilities
        c. Establishing safety rules
        d. Safety committees
        e. Inspections: OSHA, self, on-site consultations
        f. Investigations
        g. Evaluation

    2. Safety Promotion

        a. Training
        b. Communications
        c. Recognition
        d. Incentives

    3. Accident Investigation

        a. Accident scene
        b. Interviews
        c. Accident report
        d. Evaluation and follow-up

e. Research and corrective action

4. Safety Inspections

    a. Hazard identification and control
    b. Safety rule compliance
    c. Follow-up and corrective action

5. Human Factors Engineering (ergonomics)

6. Special Safety Considerations

    a. Toxic or hazardous chemicals
    b. Video display terminals

7. Sources of Assistance

D. Security (1.14%, 1.36%)

1. Organization of Security

    a. Vulnerability analysis
    b. Planning
    c. Establishing roles and responsibilities
    d. Evaluation
    e. Liability limits
    f. Protection of executives against kidnapping
    g. Threat of violence

2. Control Systems

   a. Physical security
   b. Disturbance
   c. Parking and traffic
   d. Entry systems

3. Protection of Proprietary Information

   a. Computer security
   b. Industry guidelines
   c. Patents

4. Crisis Management and Contingency Planning

5. Theft and Fraud

   a. Honesty and polygraph testing
   b. Internal financial procedures limit

6. Investigations and Preventive Corrections

# RESOURCES

The selected resources may prove useful in preparing for the Institute's certification examination. The resources are classified by each of the functional areas of the certification examination. No attempt has been made to provide an inclusive list of resources. These resources represent a solid foundation for a human resource professional library.

## Management Practices (including HR Management)

Anthony, William, Pamela Perrewe and K. Michele Kacmar, <u>Strategic Human Resource Management,</u> Chicago, IL: The Dryden Press, 1993.

Baird, Lloyd S., <u>Managing Human Resources: Integrating People and Business Strategy,</u> Irwin Professional Publishing, 1992.

Beach, Dale S., <u>Personal: The Management of People at Work,</u> 6th ed., Columbus, OH: MacMillan Publishing Company, 1994.

Bernarding, H. John, <u>Human Resources Management: An Experimental Approach,</u> New York, NY: McGraw-Hill Companies, 1992.

Byars, Lloyd L., and Leslie W. Rue, <u>Human Resource Management,</u> 4th ed., Homewood, IL: Richard D. Irwin, Inc., 1993.

Carrell, Michael R., Norbert F. Elbert and Robert D. Hatfield, Human Resource Management: Global Strategies for Managing a Diverse Work Force, Columbus, OH: MacMillan Publishing Company, 1995.

Cascio, Wayne F., Costing Human Resources: The Financial Impact of Behavior in Organizations, 3rd ed., Boston, MA: Kent Publishing Company, 1991.

Cascio, Wayne F., Managing Human Resources 3rd ed., New York, NY: McGraw-Hill Companies, 1992.

Ceriello, Vincent R., Human Resource Management Systems: Strategies, Tactics and Techniques, Lexington Books, 1992.

Cherrington, David J., The Management of Human Resources, 4th ed., Needhan Heights, MA: Allyn & Bacon, 1994.

DeCenzo, David A. and Stephen P. Robbins, Human Resource Management: Concepts and Practices, 5th ed., John Wiley & Sons, Inc., 1996.

Dessler, Gary, Human Resource Management, 6th ed., Englewood Cliffs, NJ: Prentice Hall, Inc., 1993.

Dowling, Peter J., Randall S. Schuler and Denice E. Welch, International Dimensions of Human Resource Management, 2nd ed., Wadsworth Publishing Company, 1994.

Dyer, Lee ed., <u>Human Resource Management: Evolving Roles and Responsibilities</u>, ASPA-BNA Services #1, Washington, DC: The Bureau of National Affairs, Inc., 1988.

Ferris, Gerald R. and M. Ronald Buckley, eds., <u>Human Resource Management: Perspectives, Context, Functions, and Outcomes,</u> 3rd ed., Englewood Cliffs, NJ: Prentice Hall, Inc., 1995.

Fisher, Cynthia D., Lyle Schoenfeldt, and James B. Shaw, <u>Human Resource Management</u>, 3rd ed., Houghton-Mifflin Company, 1996.

Fitz-Enz, Jac, <u>How to Measure Human Resource Management</u>, 2nd ed., New York, NY: McGraw-Hill Companies, 1995.

Fitz-Enz, Jac, <u>Human Value Management</u>, San Francisco, CA: Jossey-Bass, Inc., 1990.

French, Wendell, <u>Human Resources Management</u>, 3rd ed., Houghton-Mifflin Company, 1994.

Gomez-Mejia, Luis R., David B. Balkin and Robert L. Cardy, <u>Managing Human Resources</u>, Englewood Cliffs, NJ: Prentice Hall, 1994.

Harvey, Don and Robert B. Bowin, <u>Human Resource Management: An Experimental Approach</u>, Englewood Cliffs, NJ: Prentice Hall, 1996.

Hodgetts, Richard M. and K. Galen Kroeck, Personnel & Human Resource Management, Chicago, IL: The Dryden Press, 1992.

International HR Learning System, Society for Human Resource Management, 1994.

Ivancevich, John M., Human Resource Management, 6th ed., Homewood, IL: Richard D. Irwin, Inc., 1994.

Lewin, David and Daniel J. Mitchell Human Resource Management: An Economic Approach, 2nd ed., Cincinnati, OH: South-Western Publishing Company, 1995.

Mathis, Robert L. and John H. Jackson, Human Resource Management, 7th ed., St. Paul, MN: West Publishing Company, 1994.

Milkovich, George T. and John W. Boudreau, Personnel: Human Resource Management, 7th ed., Homewood, IL: Richard D. Irwin, Inc., 1993.

Miner, John B. and Donald P. Crane, Human Resource Management: The Strategic Perspective, Harper-Collins, 1995.

Noe, Raymond A., Human Resource Management: Gaining a Competitive Advantage, Homewood, IL: Richard D. Irwin, Inc., 1994.

Patrick, Floyd A., <u>Personnel-Human Resource Management</u>, Kendall Hunt Publishing Company, 1994.

<u>Reengineering the HR Function</u>, SHRM Foundation, 1994.

Sadler, Anthony, <u>Human Resource Management: Developing a Strategic Approach</u>, Cassell Publishing, 1995.

Scarpello, Vida G., <u>Human Resource Management: Environments & Functions</u>, 2nd ed., Cincinnati, OH: South-Western Publishing Company, 1995.

Schuler, Randall S., <u>Managing Human Resources in the Information Age</u>, SHRM-BNA Series #6, Washington, DC: The Bureau of National Affairs, Inc., 1990.

Schuler, Randall S., and Susan E. Jackson, <u>Human Resource Management: Positioning for the 21st Century</u>, 6th ed., St. Paul, MN: West Publishing Company, 1995.

Sherman, Arthur W., Jr. and George W. Bohlander, <u>Managing Human Resources</u>, Cincinnati, OH: South-Western Publishing Company, 1992.

<u>SHRM Learning System</u>, Society for Human Resource Management, 1995.

Singer, Marc G., <u>Human Resource Management</u>, PWS-Kent, 1990.

Sisson, Keith, Personnel Management, 2nd ed., Blackwell Publishers, 1994.

Torrington, Derek and Laura Hall, Personnel Management: HRM in Action, 3rd ed., Englewood Cliffs, NJ: Prentice Hall, Inc., 1995.

## Selection and Placement

Arvey, Richard D. and Roberty Faley, Fairness in Selecting Employees, 2nd ed., Reading, MA: Addison-Wesley Publishing Company, 1988.

Cascio, Wayne F., Human Resource Planning, Employement and Placement, ASPA-BNA Series #2, Washington, DC: The Bureau of National Affairs, Inc. 1989.

Frierson, James G., Employer's Guide to the Americans with Disabilities Act, Washington, DC: The Bureau of National Affairs, Inc., 1992.

Fyock, Catherine D., Get the Best, Irwin Professional Publishers, 1993.

Gatewood, Robert D. and Hubert S. Feild, Human Resource Selection, 3rd ed., Chicago, IL: The Dryden Press, 1994.

Ledvinka, James and Vida Scarpello, Federal Regulation of Personnel and Human Resource Management, Boston, MA: Kent Publishing Company, 1991.

Schneider, Benjamin and Neal Schmitt, <u>Staffing Organizations</u>, 2nd ed., Waveland Press, 1992.

Schmitt, Neal and Walter C. Borman and Associates, <u>Personnel Selection in Organizations</u>, San Francisco, CA: Jossey-Bass, Inc., 1992.

"Uniform Guidelines on Employee Selection Procedures," <u>Federal Register</u>, August 15, 1978, Part IV, 38295-38309.

## Training and Development

Kirkpatrick, Donald L. <u>How to Train and Develop Supervisors,</u> AMACOM, 1993.

Schneier, Craig Eric and Craig J. Russell, Richard W. Beatty and Lloyd S. Baird, <u>Training and Development Sourcebook</u>, 2nd ed., Amherst, MA: Human Resource Development Press, 1993.

Tracey, William R., <u>Human Resources Management and Development Handbook</u>, 2nd ed., AMACOM, 1994.

Wexley, Kenneth N., ed., <u>Developing Human Resources</u>, SHRM-BNA Series #5, Washington, DC: The Bureau of National Affairs, Inc., 1990.

## Compensation and Benefits

Dixon, R. Brian, <u>The Federal Wage and Hour Laws</u>, SHRM Foundation, 1994.

Gomez-Mejia, Luis R., ed., <u>Compensation and Benefits</u>, ASPA-BNA Series #3, Washington, DC: The Bureau of National Affairs, Inc., 1989.

Henderson, Richard I., <u>Compensation Management: Rewarding Performance</u>, 6th ed., Reston, VA: Reston Publishing Company, Inc., 1994.

Lawler, Edward E., III, <u>Strategic Pay: Aligning Organizational Strategies and Pay Systems</u>, San Francisco, CA: Jossey-Bass, Inc., 1990.

McCaffery, Robert M., <u>Employee Benefit Programs: A Total Compensation Perspective</u>, 2nd ed., Boston, MA: PWS Kent Publishing Company, 1992.

Schuster, Jay R., and Patricia K. Zingheim, <u>The New Pay: Linking Employee and Organizational Performance</u>, Lexington Books, 1992.

## Employee and Labor Relations

BNA Editorial Staff, <u>Grievance Guide</u>, 8th ed., Washington, DC: The Bureau of National Affairs, Inc., 1992.

Fossum, John, ed., <u>Employee and Labor Relations</u>, SHRM-BNA Series #4, Washington, DC: The Bureau of National Affairs, Inc., 1990.

Holley, William H., and Kenneth Jennings, <u>The Labor Relations Process</u>, 5th ed., Chicago, IL: The Dryden Press, 1994.

Kahn, Linda G., <u>Primer of Labor Relations</u>, 25th ed., Washington, DC: The Bureau of National Affairs, Inc., 1994.

Redeker, James R., <u>Employee Discipline: Policies and Practices</u>, Washington, DC: The Bureau of National Affairs, Inc., 1987.

Sloane, Arthur A. and Fred Witney, <u>Labor Relations</u>, 8th ed., Englewood Cliffs, NJ: Prentice Hall, Inc., 1993.

**Health, Safety and Security**

Blosser, Fred, <u>Primer on Occupational Safety and Health</u>, Washington, DC: The Bureau of National Affairs, Inc., 1992.

# CERTIFICATION EXAMINATIONS

The Institute's PHR and SPHR certification examinations are administered nation-wide twice a year at over 75 test centers. Both examinations consist of 250 multiple choice questions each with four possible answers. Four hours are allotted to complete the examination. A passing or cut score is determined using the expert judgments of a standards setting panel. This score will vary depending on the actual examination form utilized.

The certification examination measures an individual's mastery of the body of knowledge. Both levels of the examination cover the same functional areas, but differ in terms of the individual test items and their respective weightings. Preparation for the examination is best accomplished by mastering the application of the human resource (HR) body of knowledge.

HRCI uses exclusively four option multiple-choice items in its certification examinations for a number of reasons:

1. They are flexible and adaptable.
2. They tend to be more reliable than other formats.
3. They can accommodate a wide range of skills, knowledges and abilities to be measured.
4. They provide good sampling.
5. They have low chance scores.
6. They can be machine scored.

Multiple-choice items consist of three parts:

**Stem**                      The stem states the problem or question to be answered.

**Correct Answer**       The correct answer is one of four potential options which represents the only correct response or the best correct response. ("Best" means a panel of experts would agree to this judgment.)

**Distractors**            Three distractors serve as incorrect responses. They are plausible, yet wrong, or not the best possible option.

The following is an example of the parts of a multiple-choice item:

**Stem:**                  Typically, the most unreliable tool utilized in the selection process is a(n)

| | | |
|---|---|---|
| **Correct Answer:** | *A. | employment interview. |
| **Distractor:** | B. | selection test. |
| **Distractor:** | C. | physical examination. |
| **Distractor:** | D. | background check. |

    Items used on the Institute's certification examinations are developed by certified HR professionals who volunteer their services. These individuals are given detailed training and specific guidelines on item development.

    Once items are developed, they go through an exhaustive item review process. A separate group of certified HR professionals thoroughly scrutinize each item and perform a number of validity checks. Each remaining item is then categorized as either a PHR or SPHR item and coded to the Institute's content outline.

A final review of each examination form is conducted by the Institute's Board of Directors. Each examination form is carefully evaluated by the Board before being certified for use.

The three step process of item development, item review and validation and examination review ensures that items are:

- clear, unambiguous and grammatically proper

- technically correct

- appropriate in terms of fairness--geographically, ethnically or culturally

- important for human resource professionals to know, and

- correctly coded to the HRCI Content Outline

The PHR examinations and the SPHR examinations differ significantly in terms of the weights assigned to each of the six HR body of knowledge functional areas. Of equal importance, is the difference in focus and format of the individual items on the examinations. In general, PHR items are more technical application questions. Many are at the operational level. On the other hand, SPHR items tend to be more policy application questions. Many are at the strategic level. Additionally, there is a greater proportion of scenario questions on the SPHR examinations. A scenario question poses an HR situation followed by a series of questions based on the information supplied. Scenario questions are particularly well suited to SPHR examinees. They represent typical situations that senior level HR practitioners encounter and the diverse knowledge requirements needed to solve those situations.

Examinations are administered nationwide through a professional testing service. This organization supplies expert counsel in examination design and construction and also provides analysis of examination results.

# EXAMINATION PREPARATION METHODS, STRATEGIES, AND RESOURCES

An important issue for examinees is preparation. There are a number of methods available in preparing for the HRCI examinations. The selection of a method is a matter of individual preference based upon what best fits into one's lifestyle. Methods range from the highly informal individual self-study to highly structured courses and workshops.

Likewise, the strategy used to prepare for the certification examinations is equally important. Just like a world class athlete must "peak" at the precise moment of competition, so must an examinee on examination day. In addition to being able to master the HRCI body of knowledge, the examinee should be both mentally and physically prepared to sit for the examination. Strategy is a critical element of preparation.

The resources used to prepare are also critical elements of preparation. Sometimes the resources utilized will be a function of the preparation method selected. Other times, the potential examinee will have to select an appropriate resource from a wide range of possibilities. A mistake in selecting resources can significantly impact an examinee's score.

## **Methods**

Care must be taken in selecting a method of preparation. Because the HRCI examination measures one's mastery of the application of the HR body of knowledge, one cannot train or teach to the examination. Instead, preparation is best accomplished by knowing the HR knowledge requirements and being able to apply them. Methods which utilize the same basic format as that used by HRCI are preferable because they help familiarize the potential test taker with HRCI's organization of the body of knowledge.

HRCI serves as a standard setting and credentialing organization. As such, it does not directly provide professional development activities. SHRM's Professional Development Department can serve as a resource in surveying and selecting a preparation method.

Self-Study

Self-study can either be individual, whereby one studies at his/her own pace to suit his/her own schedule, or it can be a group experience where there are regular meetings, mutual assistance, and lively exchanges of ideas and information among members. No matter which study method is utilized, a key concept is flexibility.

Individual self-study requires a fairly high degree of personal discipline. One must develop a strategy and schedule for preparation and then stay on track. Prepackaged preparation systems such as the *SHRM Learning System* are convenient for that purpose. Also, any of the general HR references cited in this Guide can serve as a starting point for individual self-study.

A variation of individual self-study is paired self-study. This method involves the buddy system. Two examinees are matched up and utilizing the same format as with individual self-study begin the process of preparing to sit for the certification examination. It is a highly flexible method while at the same time offering the potential examinees the feeling of not "going it alone."

Group study offers some advantages over individual and paired self-study. The camaraderie and support of the group can be a great asset of preparation. Many SHRM Chapters sponsor certification study groups. Some key concepts to consider in establishing a study group are:

- convenient meeting locations and times

- a certified HR professional to serve as a mentor to the study group

- pre-and post-testing using the same examination as in this Guide

- a study format with a schedule and individual member assignments

- the use of multiple resources for preparation

Self-study, whether it is individual paired, or group, serves as an excellent preparation method when flexibility is the key consideration. HRCI has available at no cost a pamphlet entitled Guide to Certification Coordination. It provides helpful hints and sample schedules as one embarks on self-study. Although emphasizing group study, it is adaptable for individual self-study. A copy can be obtained by contacting HRCI at (703) 548-3440, fax (703) 836-0367, e-mail: hrci@shrm.org, homepage: http://www.shrm.org/docs/hrci.html.

## College and University Courses

Many colleges and universities offer courses designed to prepare HR practitioners to take the HRCI examinations. Most often these courses are offered on a non-credit/continuing education basis; however, some academic institutions allow credit for these courses.

A number of colleges and universities have entered into arrangements with SHRM to offer their certification preparation courses utilizing the SHRM Learning System. The SHRM Learning System was developed utilizing the HRCI body of knowledge outline as a blue print. Other colleges and universities use other materials. Quality of instruction and resources should be carefully scrutinized. It is always a good idea to check references with a past course participant before registering for such courses.

## SHRM Chapter Sponsored Short Courses

Many local SHRM Chapters offer short courses to assist in preparing for the HRCI examinations. These short courses provide instruction and a structured program covering the HRCI body of knowledge. Local SHRM Chapters should be contacted to determine availability of these courses in your area.

## SHRM Certification Preparation Course

Potential examinees who already have a good understanding of the HR field may be interested in the SHRM Review Course for Certification. This course serves as an intensive refresher or review of the HR body of knowledge. It is specifically designed for the experienced HR practitioners who need a refresher before the examination. It is offered nationally in selected locations prior to each of HRCI's national examination dates. Information about this

Certification Review Course can be obtained by calling the SHRM Professional Development department at 1-800-283-7476.

Private Training Organizations

Some private training organizations offer courses in preparing for the HRCI examinations. Care should be taken to ensure that the approach used in the course corresponds to the HRCI body of knowledge content outline.

If the method chosen to prepare for certification uses instructors, it is important that they be certified. It is hard, if not impossible, to adequately explain about a process that one has not gone through. Personal experiences of instructor's offer valuable insights and increase the comfort levels of examinees.

Regardless of the method used, a high degree of personal commitment is necessary for one to receive the most benefit from the preparation experience.

## **Strategies**

Any of the methods for certification preparation require the development of strategy for maximizing one's performance on the HRCI certification examination. This strategy development involves four elements -- self assessment, structuring time, mental and physical preparedness and dealing with post examination emotions.

Self-Assessment - No two examinees bring the same education, experience and preparation to the examination table. As a result, an important strategy is to conduct a honest self assessment of one's qualifications and experiences in the human resource field.

Begin by reviewing your education and experience in light of the major areas of the HRCI content outline. It might be wise to compare your resume side-by-side with the HRCI outline. What areas has your education and experience given you a strong knowledge and application base? What areas are you going to have to work on? Make a preliminary list of your strengths and weaknesses.

Next, take the Practice Examination in this <u>Certification Guide</u>. Resist the temptation to look the answers up until you have completed the examination. Now correct the practice examination and total your score by each of the six functional areas of the HRCI examination. Does your performance correspond to your own self-assessment based upon your review of your education and experience? Remember, this practice examination is only one hundred thirty-five questions and the HRCI certification examination is two hundred and fifty questions. Even though the practice examination is shorter, it still can serve as an important assessment tool.

Using these self-assessment approaches should help you focus on those areas where the most preparation is needed. Always focus on the areas where you need the most preparation based upon the weightings of the specific examination (PHR or SPHR) you have applied to take.

<u>Structuring Time</u> - Once a self-assessment has been conducted, an approach should be mapped out to maximize one's use of time in preparing for the certification examination. The approach to structuring time will be different based upon the level of examination (PHR or SPHR) and the self-assessment. The following represent sample eight, ten and twelve week schedules:

## Eight Week Schedule

### PHR Level

| Week | Topic |
|---|---|
| 1 | Introduction / Pre-Test |
| 2 | Management Practices |
| 3 | Selection & Placement |
| 4 | Training & Development |
| 5 | Compensation & Benefits |
| 6 | Comp. & Benefits / Employee & Labor Relations |
| 7 | Employee & Labor Relations |
| 8 | Health, Safety, & Security / Post-Test |

### SPHR Level

| Week | Topic |
|---|---|
| 1 | Introduction / Pre-Test |
| 2 | Management Practices |
| 3 | Management Practices |
| 4 | Selection & Placement |
| 5 | Training & Development |
| 6 | Compensation & Benefits |
| 7 | Employee & Labor Relations |
| 8 | Health, Safety, & Security / Post-Test |

## Ten Week Schedule

### PHR Level

| Week | Topic |
|---|---|
| 1 | Introduction / Pre-Test |
| 2 | Management Practices |
| 3 | Selection & Placement |
| 4 | Selection & Placement |
| 5 | Training & Development |
| 6 | Compensation & Benefits |
| 7 | Compensation & Benefits |
| 8 | Employee & Labor Relations |
| 9 | Employee & Labor Relations |
| 10 | Health, Safety, & Security/Post-Test |

### SPHR Level

| Week | Topic |
|---|---|
| 1 | Introduction / Pre-Test |
| 2 | Management Practices |
| 3 | Management Practices |
| 4 | Selection & Placement |
| 5 | Selection & Placement/Training & Development |
| 6 | Training & Development/Compensation & Benefits |
| 7 | Compensation & Benefits |
| 8 | Employee & Labor Relations |
| 9 | Employee & Labor Relations |
| 10 | Health, Safety, & Security/Post-Test |

## Twelve Week Schedule

### PHR Level

| Week | Topic |
|---|---|
| 1 | Introduction / Pre-Test |
| 2 | Management Practices |
| 3 | Management Practices |
| 4 | Selection & Placement |
| 5 | Selection & Placement |
| 6 | Training & Development |
| 7 | Training & Development |
| 8 | Compensation & Benefits |
| 9 | Compensation & Benefits |
| 10 | Employee & Labor Relations |
| 11 | Employee & Labor Relations |
| 12 | Health, Safety, & Security/Post-Test |

### SPHR Level

| Week | Topic |
|---|---|
| 1 | Introduction / Pre-Test |
| 2 | Management Practices |
| 3 | Management Practices |
| 4 | Management Practices |
| 5 | Selection & Placement |
| 6 | Selection & Placement |
| 7 | Training & Development |
| 8 | Compensation & Benefits |
| 9 | Compensation & Benefits |
| 10 | Employee & Labor Relations |
| 11 | Employee & Labor Relations |
| 12 | Health, Safety, & Security/Post-Test |

These sample schedules should be customized to your self-assessment. Maximization of preparation time is directly related to examination performance.

Mental and Physical Preparedness - A common mistake made by many examinees is cramming the week or night before the certification examination. In reality, such behavior hurts and not helps examination performance. Preparation comes best if spaced out over an extended period of time.

Given the nature of HRCI examinations, a clear head using logical thought processes will help examination performance much more than any limited knowledge gained by last minute cramming. The HRCI examinations are intellectually challenging and fatiguing. Appearing at a test site already fatigued from cramming the night before is not a wise strategy. Prepare early and relax the night before the examination. Go out to eat or to a movie the night before the examination. Get a good night's sleep and come to the exam center relaxed and alert.

Post Examination Emotions - An important element of strategy development is to deal with post examination emotions. Examinees should be aware of these emotions long before they sit for the certification examination. Two emotions are prevalent after sitting for an HRCI examination and they both deal with frustration. First, examinees are frustrated because they generally don't know how they have performed on the examination. Second, examinees are frustrated because they don't know what they could have done to perform any better on the examination. Both of these emotions are quite common for any mastery of a body of knowledge examination.

These examinations can not be taught or trained to like curriculum based examinations. Ask any examinee for the BAR, and they will express the same frustrations. Realize these frustrations early so that you will be better prepared to deal with them after the examination administration.

## **Resources**

Some preparation methods will already have identified the resources to be utilized. Other preparation methods leave it up to the prospective examinee. Therefore, selection of appropriate resources is critically important.

Because the certification exam measures mastery of the entire HR body of knowledge, there is no one best resource to use in preparation for the exam.

One effective way to understand the importance of using various resources is to imagine a giant globe filled with marbles. Each marble represents one piece of the HR body of knowledge from each of the six functional areas. Each certification exam is composed of a random drawing of marbles according to the percentage listed for each functional area on the HRCI Content Outline.

If you can visualize the giant globe filled with thousands of marbles, you can easily see that it's impossible to predict which of the marbles will end up on the exam. It is equally impossible for any one preparatory resource to contain all the marbles.

This is why the HRCI recommends using a variety of resources for the most comprehensive exposure to the HR body of knowledge.

HRCI's mission is to identify the HR body of knowledge and to develop an instrument to measure mastery of this knowledge. It is not to develop resources to teach the body of knowledge and to test examinees on their mastery of knowledge contained in such a resource.

To maintain exam integrity, the HRCI separates itself from the development of preparatory resources and does not endorse any one particular resource. Below is a partial list of resources available; please refer to the resources following the HRCI Content Outline in this Certification Guide.

- **The SHRM Learning System** covers all six functional areas of the content outline and includes self-directed modules, application activities, and end-of-module examinations. It was designed to follow the body of knowledge content outline and is available from SHRM.

- **The SHRM-BNA Series** is a six-part handbook series on human resource management. This series is not often used as a single exam preparation source, but the individual handbooks are a good way for individuals to focus on areas in which they need more extensive preparation.

- **HR Textbooks are a good resource.** Be sure to select textbooks that are up-to-date, since the HR body of knowledge changes rapidly. Resources more than one or two years old should be used only with great caution. It is also recommended that several texts be used, rather than just one, so that different perspectives are gained and nothing is overlooked.

- **Custom-designed resources** are used by some SHRM chapters and proprietary companies. Many of these resources are not original works, but are committee-assembled compilations of other resources.

- **Lending Libraries** are popular with some SHRM chapters. Learning resources are purchased and made available to chapter members at no cost or with a nominal fee. This allows members to review materials they may not otherwise be able to afford.

# EXAMINATION TAKING SKILLS

It is natural for anyone approaching an examination to have some anxieties and nervousness. The anxiety level is likely to be even higher for individuals who have been out of school for several years.

All of the questions on the HRCI examinations are multiple-choice in nature. The question statement is called the <u>stem</u> and the answers are called <u>choices</u>. Some of the choices are designed to be plausible but incorrect, and they are called <u>distracters</u>.

Questions on the exam are different types, especially at the PHR level. Some will be <u>identification</u>, which means that definitions of concepts or facts are being tested. Also, <u>relationship</u> questions are used to test how one concept is related to or affects another one. Other questions are <u>application</u> in nature, in which a situation is posed and the choices reflect applying certain facts to the situation.

Below are some test-taking suggestions that may aid you in performing up to your capabilities and knowledge.

1. <u>Mark on the test booklet.</u> The test booklet is for you to use to take the test. Therefore, mark on it by making short notes, doing simple calculations, placing an $\underline{x}$ by implausible answers, and putting question marks by questions you do not answer the first time through the exam.

2. <u>Trust your first impressions.</u> There is a correct answer to each question. It is widely believed that your first impression of the correct answer will be a better choice.

3. **Avoid over analyzing.** Be careful that you do not "read" too much into an answer.

4. **Answer the questions in order.** Because the exam is structured with the easier questions at the beginning, answering these questions will give you more confidence as you proceed to the more difficult ones.

5. **If uncertain, leave blank and return.** If you cannot decide on an answer, mark the question in the margin of the exam booklet and return to it after attempting to answer all of the questions on the exam. It is possible that later questions may trigger information useful for those "undecided" questions.

6. **Don't stop.** If you are stumped by a question, continue on to the next item. Otherwise, you may lose valuable time and rush through the more difficult questions at the end of the exam.

7. **Don't look for answer patterns.** The psychometric testing process used by the Institute ensures that questions do not fall into patterns. Contrary to some myths, "c" will not necessarily be the most frequent answer, and the first answer may be correct.

8. **Length of an answer is a false clue.** One test-taking myth is that the longer an answer, the more likely it is to be correct. However, it often is more difficult to write incorrect distracters than the correct answer, so it is just as likely that the longest answer is incorrect as it is correct.

9. **Eliminate obvious distracters.** For most questions there are two distracters that usually appear to be incorrect, one that is likely to be plausible but incorrect, and then one correct answer. When you first read a question, you generally should be able to eliminate two of the answers as incorrect. If you cannot decide between the other two,

then move on to the next question and return to the unanswered question later.

10. <u>Identify your answer before reading the choices.</u> After reading the question, try to identify what you believe the answer will be before reading the choices. By doing this, you will more likely have one answer stand out as being correct.

11. <u>Use "educated guesses".</u> If you still cannot decide on a correct answer after eliminating one or two choices, choose one anyway. There is no penalty for guessing on the exam.

12. <u>Don't worry about what you don't know.</u> If you don't know the answer to a question, don't continue to fret over it and let it affect your approaching other questions positively.

13. <u>Review your answers.</u> After going through all the questions on the exam, go back and answer the questions you omitted the first time. Also, be sure that you answered all questions and that you marked the appropriate answers to each question.

14. <u>Don't rush.</u> You do not receive more points for finishing first; use the time allowed for the exam to the extent you need so that you give yourself sufficient time to review and check your answers. Also, someone who finishes early may know less than you do, so don't feel self-conscious about being among the last one to turn in your exam.

15. <u>Don't worry after the test.</u> Many people feel drained and inadequate after taking a long exam. That feeling is not necessarily directly related to doing poorly on the exam.

## CERTIFICATION EXAMINATION
## PRACTICE ITEMS

These Certification Examination Practice Items are designed to familiarize prospective examinees with the style and format of the HRCI examination questions. The 135 practice items are arranged by each of the functional areas of the HRCI Outline. These items are arranged in this manner to facilitate scoring and self-assessment.

The actual HRCI certification examinations are 250 items. **(Note: the items are randomly arranged on the HRCI examination forms and not in functional areas as they appear here.)**

None of these items will be found on the HRCI certification examination. These practice items are only meant to be representative of the type of items found in certification examinations. Following the practice items in each functional area are the correct answers, rationales for the answers and HRCI Content Outline coding.

Remember to circle the <u>BEST</u> answer. Good luck!

## **MANAGEMENT PRACTICES - ITEMS**

1.  For which position would an employer most likely be able to support a BFOQ based upon sex?

    a. Sportscaster
    b. Locker room attendant
    c. Nurse
    d. OB-GYN physician

2. Which single document meets all the requirements of the Immigration and Naturalization Service's Form I-9?

   a:  A state-issued drivers license
   b.  A social security card
   c.  A birth certificate
   d.  A United States passport

3. Which of the following questions asked during an interview would most likely give rise to an inference of discrimination?

   a.  Describe your military experience.
   b.  Do you have a job-related disability?
   c.  To what professional organizations do you belong?
   d.  Describe the extracurricular activities you did in college.

4. In order to avoid a charge of negligent hiring, an employer should give special attention to which phase of a selection system?

   a.  Interviewing
   b.  Honesty testing
   c.  Reference checking
   d.  Medical examinations

5. What is the first response by the EEOC after a charge of discrimination has been filed?

   a.  Conduct an investigation
   b.  Issue a right to sue letter
   c.  Attempt conciliation
   d.  Attempt a no fault predetermination settlement

6. All employees with _____ or more employees, must file an annual EEO-I (or I-VI) with the EEOC.

   a. 15
   b. 20
   c. 50
   d. 100

7. An organization hired 50 management trainees, and the selection rate for non-minorities was 25%. If 30 minorities apply, how many minorities should be hired to avoid an adverse impact claim?

   a. 3
   b. 6
   c. 9
   d. 12

8. If the OFCCP conducted an audit of an organization's affirmative action plan for women under Revised Order 4, which factor would they give little weight to in an underutilization calculation?

   a. The availability of day care or nursery schools in the contractor's area
   b. The size of the female unemployment force in the surrounding labor area
   c. The general availability of women having requisite skills in the immediate labor area
   d. The percentage of the female work force as compared with the total work force in the immediate labor area

9. Which of the following statements best describes diversity programs?

    a. Lawful reverse discrimination
    b. Valuing differences
    c. Assimilating differences
    d. Required for government contractors

10. What best describes the content of job specifications?

    a. Essential job functions
    b. Description of work activities
    c. Job description summary
    d. Personal requirements or qualifications for performing a job

11. How could the heavy use of employee referrals for job vacancies violate nondiscrimination laws?

    a. By minority employees refusing to refer job applicants
    b. Where it results in an undesirable status quo of an under represented workforce
    c. Where minority employees constitute the majority of employees in the workforce
    d. Where an Affirmative Action Plan is not required to correct an imbalance

12. If a candidate is recruited and hired through two professional employment agency contacts and both agencies claim the fee for the referral, what is the best approach to settling the claims?

   a. Pay the fee at 50% of each agency since both made the referral
   b. Pay the full fee to each agency, since both agencies referred the candidate
   c. Recommend the two agencies negotiate the fee, since only one fee is to be paid
   d. Examine the referral documents as to dates referred and pay the fee to the agency whose referral was received first

13. If the job specifications for a certain job qualify twice as many whites as blacks, the specifications are

   a. BFOQ's.
   b. illegal.
   c. discriminatory.
   d. in need of validation.

14. To measure total organizational hiring costs, which of the following is most appropriate to consider?

   a. Only budgeted expenditures
   b. Direct out-of-pocket expenditures
   c. Both indirect and direct costs
   d. Cost data supplied by the Department of Labor

15. In the selection process, a false positive represents

 a. an unqualified candidate who was hired.
 b. a qualified candidate who was denied employment.
 c. an unqualified candidate who was denied employment.
 d. a qualified candidate who was employed.

16. A weighted application form is most appropriate for which type of position?

 a. Top level executive positions
 b. Multiple incumbent positions
 c. Positions which have underutilization of minorities
 d. Unskilled positions

17. It is not discriminatory during preemployement inquiries to inquire about an applicant's record on

 a. worker's compensation.
 b. driving.
 c. arrests.
 d. favoring unions.

18. An applicant, who was previously fired for misconduct by another employer, does not list that employment experience on the application form and is subsequently hired. One month later, this omission is discovered. How should this situation be handled?

 a. The incident should be overlooked and considered a casual omission.

b. The employee should receive a written disciplinary letter over the incident.
c. The employee should be fired for falsification of the application.
d. The previous employer should be contacted to determine the cause of the prior dismissal.

19. Realistic job previews

    a. increase turnover during the first year of employment.
    b. lead to more refusals of job offers.
    c. make recruitment advertising more factual.
    d. typically do not deal with the organizational realities of the position.

20. Which type of interview has the most potential for valid selection?

    a. Directive
    b. Non-directive
    c. Structured
    d. Stress

21. The use of an aptitude test in a selection program best predicts

    a. skill level.
    b. job knowledge.
    c. manual dexterity.
    d. training performance.

22. Why are skill tests more accurate in predicting failures than successes?

    a. They assess "can do" rather than "will do".
    b. The scores are more reliable in lower ranges than higher ranges.
    c. If applicants fail a test there is no certainty they will be unsuccessful on the job.
    d. They are designed to eliminate potential failures rather than identify potential successes.

23. A selection test for fire fighters which requires all applicants to pull a 90 pound hose up three flights of stairs within a four minute period would suggest which type of validity?

    a. Predictive
    b. Concurrent
    c. Content
    d. Construct

24. The most adequate defense an employer has in a defamation of character law suit arising from providing reference information is

    a. the absence of malice.
    b. that the information given was the truth.
    c. that the employer had a qualified privilege to provide the information.
    d. that the employee signed a release.

25. A medical examination as part of the selection process should be

    a.    conducted prior to making the selection decision.
    b.    scheduled after an employment offer has been extended.
    c.    eliminated as a result of the Americans With Disabilities Act.
    d.    conducted on a random basis.

127

## MANAGEMENT PRACTICES
## ANSWERS, RATIONALES, CODING

1.  Answer: b.   Locker room attendant

    A Bona Fide Occupational Qualification (BFOQ) is a limited exception to the anti-bias rules available under the Civil Rights Act, the Age Discrimination in Employment Act and the Americans with Disabilities Act. A BFOQ may be established on the basis of religion, sex, or national origin or absence of disability if the requirement is necessary to the normal operation of an employer's business. This is a strict burden of proof which falls upon the employer. It is not available with respect to race or color. The locker room attendant requires monitoring of locker rooms designated for one sex. Based upon community standards, a specific sex could probably be specified and supported.

    CODE: II-A-I

2.  Answer: d.   A United States passport

    Proof of both identity and right to work are required on INS Form I-9. The U.S. passport is the only option satisfying both requirements.

    CODE: II-A-8

3.  Answer: b.   Do you have a job-related disability?

    Under the Americans With Disabilities Act (ADA), preemployment inquiries regarding a disability are unlawful. The ADA requires a focus on essential job functions and whether the person can perform those functions with or without reasonable accommodations.

CODE: II-A-12

4. Answer: c.   Reference checking

Negligent hiring is a tort law theory which states if an employer hires an employee, and the employer knew or should have known about a prior behavior of the employee which could cause harm to a third party, then the employer is liable if the employee subsequently causes harm to someone. Negligent hiring makes it extremely important for employers to thoroughly check background references on all employees who are in a position of trust or where their actions could harm others.

CODE: II-A-13-b

5. Answer: d.   Attempt a no fault predetermination settlement

The EEOC upon receiving a charge, serves it to the employer and attempts a no fault predetermination settlement. If the parties agree to the settlement, the charge is considered withdrawn by the EEOC.

CODE: II-B

6. Answer: d.   100

The EEOC requires all employers with 100 or more employees to annually file an EEO-I Report. The report numbers vary by type of organization.

| EEO-1 | Private Business |
| EEO-2 | Joint Apprenticeship Committees |
| EEO-3 | Unilateral Apprenticeship Programs |
| EEO-4 | State and Local Governments |
| EEO-5 | Public Elementary and Secondary Schools |
| EEO-6 | Colleges and Universities |

CODE: II-B-2-b

7. Answer: b.   6

Adverse impact results when the selection rate for minority group members is less than 80% (or 4/5's) of the selection rate for majority group members. In this example, the selection rate for minority group members would have to be 80% of 25% or 20% of 30 applicants (6).

CODE: II-B-2-d

8. Answer: a.   The availability of day care or nursery schools in the contractor's area

The OFCCP requires an eight factor analysis to determine availability of protected group members (PGM). The eight factors are:

1. the PGM population of the labor area surround the facility;
2. the size of the PGM unemployment force or labor area surrounding the facility;
3. the percentage of PGM as compared to the total workforce in the immediate labor area;
4. the availability of PGM with requisite skills in the immediate labor area;
5. the availability of PGM with requisite skills in the area from which the contractor can reasonably recruit;
6. the availability of promotable and transferable PGM in the contractor's organization;
7. the existence of training facilities in the area; and,
8. the degree of training the contractor can undertake.

Child or day care facilities, although important, are not one of the eight factors considered by the OFCCP.

CODE: II-B-3-c

9. Answer: b.   Valuing differences

Diversity programs help employees understand, appreciate and value others who may be different than themselves. It represents a culture change away from ethnocentrism and exclusivity toward inclusiveness and community.

CODE: II-B-4-a

131

10. Answer: d. Personal requirements or qualifications for performing a job

Job specifications include the knowledge, skills and abilities necessary to perform a job. All other options deal with what an employee is required to do, not the qualifications necessary to do them.

CODE: II-C-2-c

11. Answer: b. Where it results in an undesirable status quo of an under represented workforce

Recruitment by "word of mouth" through current employees may create EEO problems. An under represented workforce will usually refer applicants like the work force itself. The effect of such recruitment is to perpetuate past discrimination.

CODE: II-C-3-b

12. Answer: d. Examine the referral documents as to dates referred and pay the fee to the agency whose referral was received first

Although the other options all seem plausible, the HR manager is faced with an issue of contract law. The rule of thumb is that the first to refer receives the fee. Most agency contracts contain language to that effect.

CODE: II-C-4-e

132

13. Answer: d. In need of validation

According to the Uniform Guidelines for Employee Selection Procedures, any employment tool or mechanism which results in adverse impact must be validated. Selection criteria should be job related and content validated through a job analysis.

CODE: II-C-2-c

14. Answer: c. Both indirect and direct costs

In calculating total organizational hiring costs, all costs associated with the turnover must be considered. Down time, lost productivity, training time, etc. are a few of the cost factors which must be considered.

CODE: II-C-5-c

15. Answer: a. An unqualified candidate who was hired

A false positive is when an applicant does well on a selection device, but subsequently is unsuccessful on the job. A false negative is when an applicant does poorly on a selection device, yet would have been successful if hired. Neither represents predictability.

CODE: II-D

16. Answer: b. Multiple incumbent positions

Weighted applications are designed using job analysis and performance appraisal data. Weights or numerical scores are placed on certain responses on the application based upon performance data. Weighted applications are time consuming and must be periodically validated the same as tests. Because of this fact, they are most appropriate for multiple incumbent positions.

CODE: II-D-1-c

17. Answer: b.   Driving

Inquiries regarding a driving record is legitimate if the future employee has to drive as part of his or her duties. Inquiries regarding worker's compensation may be illegal under the ADA. Inquiries on arrest records have a disproportionate impact on minority group members. Employers may not discriminate based upon union preference.

CODE: II-D-1-e

18. Answer: c.   The employee should be fired for falsification of the application

A commonly recognized principal at law is that fraudulent misrepresentation on an application form is grounds for immediate dismissal. Additionally, falsification of official records is viewed as a serious violation of work rules. If an applicant intentionally lies or conceals information and was previously terminated by another employer for misconduct, one can assume more problems will occur. The best indicator of future performance is past performance. The employee should be terminated.

CODE: II-D-1-e

19. Answer: b.   Lead to more refusals of job offers

A realistic job preview (RJP) is the process whereby an employment interviewer provides an applicant with an extremely accurate picture of the job. It is, in a sense, a "truth in employment" process. Applicants are provided both the good and bad aspects of the job to aid in the matching process. As a result, employers generally have more job offer refusals. However, once employed, turnover is usually lower with a RJP.

CODE: II-D-2

20. Answer: c.   Structured

A structured interview involves asking the same basic questions of all the applicants. It provides consistent data on which to evaluate the applicants and consequently has the most potential for valid selection.

CODE: II-D-2-c

21. Answer: d.   Training performance

An aptitude test measures accumulated learning from a number of sources. It measures a person's capability which is related to training performance. Other tests are more appropriate at predicting the other options.

CODE: II-D-3-a

22. Answer: a.   They measure "can do" rather than "will do"

Performance is a function of skills and abilities times motivation. Skill tests measure whether the person has the skills necessary to perform the job. They measure aptitude which in turn serves as a measure of capability. Skill tests do not predict motivation, therefore they are better at predicting failures rather than successes.

CODE: II-D-3-a

23. Answer: c.   Content

Pulling a 90 pound hose up three flights of stairs represents an actual work sample for a fire fighter. Work samples are the most basic form of content validity. The test in this instance measures an actual content domain of the job.

CODE: II-D-3-h

24. Answer: b.   That the information given was the truth

The ultimate or absolute defense in a defamation of character suit is the truth. In order for a plaintiff to prevail, he or she must first show that the information provided was a lie. Although the other options to this item are defenses, the truth provides the most protection for the employer.

CODE: II-D-4-c

25. Answer: b. Scheduled after an employment offer has been extended

The Americans With Disabilities Act prohibits medical examinations prior to the extension of an employment offer. Results of a medical examination can then be used in making reasonable accommodations.

CODE: II-D-5-c

## **SELECTION AND PLACEMENT - ITEMS**

1. Which of the following positions is considered an HR specialist?

    a. Industrial Relations Director
    b. Human Resource Manager
    c. Personnel Administrator
    d. Human Resource Team Leader

2. What is the most effective form of upward communication?

    a. Suggestion systems
    b. Employee petitions
    c. Grievance procedures
    d. Direct discussions between supervisors and employees

3. When conducting an environmental scan, supply and demand for specific skills, changes in competitors practices and unemployment levels are all examples of which of the following influences?

    a. Geographic
    b. Governmental
    c. Labor market
    d. Union

4. The most difficult problem in forecasting demand for employees is

    a. forecasting internal supply.
    b. estimating turnover patterns.

c. determining the supply of human resources.
d. determining the relationship between personnel demand and the firms output.

5. Skills inventories are primarily used for

   a. job analysis documentation.
   b. human resource planning.
   c. setting performance standards.
   d. performance appraisals.

6. The first step in establishing an HRIS is to

   a. develop the data base.
   b. determine the information needs.
   c. establish a security and control system.
   d. select between PC and mainframe applications.

7. In a matrix organizational structure

   a. employees have three or more supervisors.
   b. two organizational structures exist at the same time.
   c. productivity is enhanced because of strict functional accountability.
   d. line authority is strengthened.

8. If a group is highly cohesive, the individuals in the group are more likely to

   a. play devil's advocate with each other.
   b. value group norms and goals.
   c. exhibit dysfunctional competition with group members.

d. desire a strong automatic leadership style.

9. Major changes to supporting cultures in mature organizations should occur

   a. regularly once very 5 years to keep pace with competitors.
   b. with each new yearly business cycle.
   c. infrequently, no more than once every 7-10 years.
   d. rarely, only once or twice during the organization's life cycle in order to minimize the negative effects of change.

10. The HR control process is normally thought of as containing the following steps: I.) comparing actual with expected performance; II.) observing and measuring performance; III.) setting expectations or standards; and IV.) taking corrective action. What is the proper sequence of these steps?

    a. I, II, III, IV
    b. II, I, IV, III
    c. IV, II, III, I
    d. III, II, I, IV

11. If an HR practitioner developed an economic or statistical model to identify costs and benefits associated with an HR program, this would be called a(n)

    a. HR audit.
    b. human resource accounting.
    c. break-even analysis.
    d. utility analysis.

12. An HR audit is:

   a. an attempt to quantify the value of its human resources to the organization.
   b. an aggregate skills inventory of the organization's human resources.
   c. a formal research effort to evaluate the current state of human resource management within the organization.
   d. a part of a human resource accounting system.

13. Which of the following constitutes an intrinsic reward?

   a. Pay
   b. Working conditions
   c. The job itself
   d. Complimentary supervision

14. Which motivation theory could directly support paying high performing incumbents more than incumbents in the same job who perform at lower levels in order to motivate effort?

   a. Need hierarchy
   b. Equity
   c. Motivation-hygiene
   d. Expectancy

15. An employee reports to work one morning with a weird hair style in order to impress the supervisor. The supervisor ignores this new hair style with the expectation that it will not be repeated. What type of behavior modification strategy was employed?

   a. Extinction

b. Punishment
c. Negative reinforcement
d. Positive reinforcement

16. The thought that leaders have a set of identifiable personality characteristics is key to which leadership approach?

   a. Situational
   b. Behavioral
   c. Style
   d. Trait

17. Leadership research has identified two major leader behaviors; one of which focuses on people and interpersonal relationships. What is the focus of the other?

   a. Power and authority
   b. Task accomplishment
   c. Organizational culture
   d. Profitability and financial accountability

18. What is the most important factor contributing to success of a TQM program in an organization?

   a. Organizational culture supports the TQM program
   b. Union acceptance of the TQM program
   c. Statistical aptitude of supervisors in quality control
   d. Individual rather than group awards for performance

19. Which of the following organization problems is best addressed through Quality Circles?

    a. Union problems
    b. Production problems
    c. EEO compliance problems
    d. Personnel problems

20. Job enrichment and job enlargement are two means of enhancing jobs through job design. What is the basic difference between the two techniques?

    a. Enriching a job involves adding more tasks to a job while enlarging a job involves adding more responsibilities
    b. Enlarging a job indicates an increased rate of pay will accompany the new job responsibilities
    c. Enlarging a job involves adding more tasks at the same level while enriching a job involves adding more responsibilities
    d. The two terms mean the same, there is no basic difference between them

21. The total span of possible work hours in a flex-time environment is referred to as

    a. core time.
    b. bandwidth time.
    c. compressed work time.
    d. contingent time.

143

22. A safety manager who wanted to know if financial incentives would reduce accidents, randomly selected two departments and offered employees bonuses for reducing accidents. The incidence rates of these two departments were compared with other departments. This study illustrates what kind of experiment?

    a.    Case study
    b.    Laboratory study
    c.    Field experiment
    d.    Simulation

23. In a normal distribution, approximately what percent of all the numbers will be within one standard deviation of the mean?

    a.    34%
    b.    50%
    c.    68%
    d.    84%

24. In developing an international HR program, which factor is most critical to the success of an expatriate assignment in a foreign country?

    a.    Equalizing negative tax consequences
    b.    Adaptation of spouse and family to a foreign country
    c.    Providing for security of expatriate and family
    d.    Readjustment training upon repatriation

25. Which of the following presents the least ethical dilemma for an HR manager to address?

   a. Specifically excluding salaries of low paying organizations from a survey of HR positions
   b. Referring a qualified personal friend's resume for an open position in another department
   c. Informing employees of the reasons for the dismissal of a co-worker
   d. Discussing an injured employee's medical condition with co-workers

## SELECTION AND PLACEMENT
## ANSWERS, RATIONALES, CODING

1.     Answer: a.    Industrial Relations Director

   An Industrial Relations Director is responsible for only labor relations and safety functions. The other positions are responsible for all major HR functions.

   CODE:    I-A-4

2.     Answer: d.    Direct discussions between supervisors and employees

   Personal communication between employees and supervisors has proven to be the most effective upward communication format. Research has shown that competent first-line supervisors are critical for management to "feel the pulse" of the organization. While the other forms of upward communications may be valuable, they are less effective than personal communications between supervisors and employees.

   CODE:    I-A-6-c

3.     Answer: c.    Labor market

   All of the options are areas generally searched in an environmental scan. The three factors listed are all factors of the relevant labor market.

   CODE:    I-B-1-d

4. Answer: d. Determining the relationship between personnel demand and the firm's output

   The demand for human resources is often directly related to the expected demand for the firm's products and/or services. In addition, the organization's objectives and productivity are important determinants.

   CODE: I-B-2-a

5. Answer: b. Human resource planning

   An employee skills inventory is a compilation of data on the skills and characteristics of employees. Skills inventories are used in human resource planning as part of the internal analysis of the organization. Typically an employee skills inventory will include individual employee demographics, career progression and performance data.

   CODE: I-B-3-a

6. Answer: b. Determine the information needs

   An HRIS supports organizational decision-making, therefore, the first step is to determine the specific information needs. The other options although important always follow the information needs analysis.

   CODE: I-B-4-a

7. Answer: b. Two organizational structures exist at the same time

With a matrix organizational structure two organizational structures exist at the same time --- conventional functional organization and a project team organization. Employees join a project team but retain their positions in the conventional organization. Matrix structures are often prevalent in new product development.

CODE: I-C-1-f

8. Answer: b. Value group norms and goals

Cohesive groups value group norms and goals sometimes in detrimental ways such as the "Group think" phenomena. However, a cohesive group is generally easier to lead to goal attainment.

CODE: I-C-2-c

9. Answer: c. Infrequently, once every 7-10 years

Changes to organizational culture should not be undertaken often. Such changes should be well-researched, planned and implemented over a period of years. This is especially true for more stable organizations with mature cultures. Usually cultural changes in such organizations take a considerable amount of time.

CODE: I-C-2-d

10. Answer: d. III, II, I, IV

Much like setting the temperature on a thermostat, the HR control process involves setting expectations/standards, observing/measuring performance, comparing actual to expected performance and taking corrective action if necessary.

CODE: I-D-2

11. Answer: d. Utility analysis

A utility analysis builds an economic or statistical model to identify the costs and benefits associated with specific HR programs or activities. Utility analysis is one of the more basic ways of establishing the worth of HR programs.

CODE: I-D-3

12. Answer: c. A formal research effort to evaluate the current state of human resources management within the organization

An HR Audit is a systematic study of the HR functions performed or not performed in the organization identifying strengths, weaknesses and corrective action.

CODE: I-D-3-b

13. Answer: c. The job itself

Motivation can be categorized as extrinsic or intrinsic. Extrinsic motivation comes from the environment -- pay, working conditions and supervision. Intrinsic motivation comes from within the employee --- the work, challenge, and curiosity.

CODE:    I-E

14.   Answer: d.   Expectancy

Expectancy theory states that an individual has the highest motivation to put forth the greatest effort if he/she believes the effort will lead to good performance and that the good performance will lead to attainment of goals.

CODE:    I-E-1-a

15.   Answer: a.   Extinction

Extinction is the ignoring of a behavior. Punishment would include sending the employee home until the hair style is changed. Negative reinforcement would exist if the supervisor criticized the hair style. Positive reinforcement would involve the supervisor complimenting the employee on the hair style.

CODE:    I-E-1-d

16.   Answer: d.   Trait

The trait leadership approach believes that all leaders possess certain personality traits. Under this approach leaders are born not made. Every leader has a set of personal traits which impacts the leadership situation.

CODE:    I-F-1-a

17. Answer: b. Task accomplishment

This item comes from the leadership research of (1) the Ohio State researchers who identified two leader behaviors of consideration and initiating structure, (2) the University of Michigan researchers who identified production-centered and employee-centered leadership, and (3) the Blake and Mouton Managerial Grid which uses as its dimensions concerns for the task and concern for people.

CODE: I-F-1-b

18. Answer: a. Organizational culture supports the TQM program

Research has shown the number one determinant of the success of a Total Quality Management program is that it is embraced by all members of the organization. TQM is not a single technique but a total philosophy for operating an organization. Although union acceptance of the TQM program and statistical aptitude of supervisors are factors which can impact success, they are far less important than organizational culture support.

CODE: I-G-4

19. Answer: b. Production problems

Quality circles are a participatory technique whereby selected work groups meet regularly to consider specific problems and recommendations for a solution to be presented to management. They best deal with problems involving production and are not well suited for people problems.

CODE: I-H-1-b

20. Answer: c. Enlarging a job involves adding more tasks at the same level while enriching a job means adding more responsibilities

Job enlargement is generally considered an increase in the number and variety of tasks in a job. It is also known as horizontal loading because the new tasks are at the same responsibility level as the previous tasks. Job enrichment involves adding more and often higher levels of responsibility to a job. It generally increases a worker's degree of control, planning, execution and evaluation of work. It is also known as vertical loading.

CODE: I-H-2

21. Answer: b. Bandwidth time

Bandwidth time refers to the total range of hours where employees may begin and end work. Core time refers to those hours where all employees must be at work. If an employee must work eight hours between 6 AM and 6 PM, the time between 6 AM and 6 PM is referred to as bandwidth time.

CODE: I-H-6-a

22. Answer: c. Field experiment

A field experiment involves manipulating an independent variable (financial incentives) and measuring the effect on a dependent variable (incident rates). A case study involves analyzing an event and describing what happened. A laboratory study and a simulation both occur in a controlled environment as opposed to a natural work environment.

CODE:    I-I-1-b

23.    Answer: c.    68%

A normal distribution is referred to as a normal bell shaped curve. It illustrates the generality that most characteristics when occurring in large numbers will group themselves around a middle value and exhibit a central tendency. Statistical inference is based upon a normal bell shaped curve. A normal bell shaped curve has perfect symmetry, has a point of inflection where the slope of the curve changes (the mean, median, and mode), and at its base each end of the curve approaches closer and closer to the base line until informity.

The standard deviation of the data from the average bears a fixed relationship in a normal curve. Plus or minus one standard deviation encompasses 68.27% of the data. Plus or minus two standard deviations includes 95.45% of the data. Plus or minus three standard deviations includes 99.7% of the data are under the curve. Most statistical inference in HR research is based upon the normal bell-shaped curve.

CODE:    I-I-2-b

24.    Answer: b.    Adaptation of spouse and family to a foreign country

Although many factors impact the success of a foreign assignment, research has consistently shown that adjustment of spouse and family is the most critical factor. Too often, employers do not give enough weight to this factor in developing their international HR programs. The focus tends to be on the expatriate and not his or her family.

CODE: I-J-3-d

25. Answer: b. Referring a qualified personal friend's resume for an open position in another department

Although all the options represent potential ethical dilemmas for the HR manager, referring the resume of a qualified friend to an open position in another department presents the least problem. As long as the HR manager does not advocate for the selection of the friend, no ethics violation would occur. To deny the referral based upon friendship would deny a qualified candidate equal opportunity. The skewing of salary survey data for self-betterment is clearly an ethics violation. Likewise, breaches of confidentiality are ethics violations.

CODE: I-K-1-b

## TRAINING AND DEVELOPMENT - ITEMS

1.  In order to prevail in a charge of discrimination based upon selecting participants for a training program, it is most appropriate for the organization to

    a.  establish a quota system to insure minority representation.
    b.  ensure the selection of trainees is well-documented and does not result in adverse impact.
    c.  utilize a self-nomination method of selecting participants.
    d.  use diversity training as the initial phase of the training program.

2.  In conducting a cost/benefit analysis of a training program, costs are often broken down into direct and indirect costs. Which of the following represents an indirect cost?

    a.  Participants' salary
    b.  Training department's overhead
    c.  Participants' lost production
    d.  Trainer's salary

3.  Training objectives should be derived from

    a.  a top management directives.
    b.  a needs analysis.
    c.  individual career plans of employees.
    d.  supervisor requests.

4. In planning for training and development, we must first determine:

    a. The available training programs
    b. Training needs
    c. The available funds for training programs
    d. The number of individuals to be trained

5. To ensure that of a job training program is valid, a trainer will emphasize

    a. conducting a job/task analysis.
    b. observing and interviewing the most productive incumbents in a job.
    c. surveying what programs are commercially available in the specific job area.
    d. outlining the traits necessary to perform the job.

6. Which type psychological test measures a person's overall ability to learn?

    a. Aptitude
    b. Interest
    c. Personality
    d. Specific abilities

7. Another term for "whole learning" is:

    a. Active practice
    b. Spaced practice
    c. Gestalt learning
    d. Immediate confirmation

8.  Research supports the concept that individuals learn best when they are

    a.  told the material's importance.
    b.  fearful of the consequences of not learning.
    c.  in a compatible group.
    d.  actively involved in the learning process.

9.  With limited exceptions, what is generally stated about the slope of a learning curve?

    a.  It is generally unpredictable
    b.  It rises faster during early stages of learning and more slowly as training continues
    c.  It rises slowly at the start of training and more rapidly as training continues
    d.  It rises at the same rate throughout training

10. In transactional analysis terminology, behavior changes through which ego state?

    a.  Adult
    b.  Parent
    c.  Little professor
    d.  Natural child

11. Which action could improve the effectiveness of assessment centers in selecting employees from within the firm for higher level positions?

    a.  Self-nomination
    b.  Greater emphasis on interpersonal skills

c. Greater use of staff T&D people
d. Minimal participation by line managers

12. A person who is thinking, "This idiot doesn't know what he or she is talking about" while listening to a lecturer is probably engaging in what form of listening?

   a. Non-listening
   b. Marginal
   c. Evaluative
   d. Projective

13. Trainees are more receptive to learning when

   a. management expresses the importance of learning.
   b. it is reinforced by their co-workers.
   c. the material learned is important to them.
   d. are fearful of the consequences of not learning.

14. Each of the following methods is on-the-job training except:

   a. Internships
   b. Apprenticeships
   c. Vestibule training
   d. Coaching

15. The in-basket training technique would be most applicable to which group of employees?

   a. Managerial
   b. Nonexempt office
   c. Production
   d. Service

16. Which of the following methods of organizational development has been criticized for the emotional stress it creates for some participants?

   a. Team building
   b. Transactional analysis
   c. Sensitivity training
   d. Survey feedback

17. In order to reduce information overload, orientation programs should

   a. be modularized and spread out over a period of time.
   b. be conducted only after an employee has served on the job for a specified period of time.
   c. include a detailed employee reference manual for later use.
   d. be presented entirely on the employees first day of employment when they have no other concerns.

18. In training supervisors for handling discipline and discharge incidents, which of the following is the most appropriate training method?

   a. On-the-job
   b. Case study
   c. Programmed instruction
   d. Role-play

19. A combination of on-the-job training and classroom training which emphasizes specific skill development is called:

    a. Internship training
    b. Laboratory training
    c. Apprenticeship training
    d. Simulation training

20. In a firm's training and development program, the trainee must believe that improved skills will lead to desired outcomes and that his or her effort in the training program will result in improved skills. These assumptions are related to which theory of motivation?

    a. Expectancy theory
    b. Reinforcement theory
    c. Motivation-hygiene theory
    d. Equity theory

21. Which training method uses videotapes to illustrate how mangers function in various situations?

    a. Business games
    b. Simulations
    c. In-basket training
    d. Behavior modeling

22. Which of the following training methods would be most appropriate to use to help a new manager develop planning and conceptual skills?

    a. Sensitivity training
    b. Human relations training

c. Simulation training
d. Role-play training

23. The concept of trainee involvement and immediate feedback are most prominent in which of the following training methods?

   a. Lecture
   b. Correspondence courses
   c. Programmed instruction
   d. Audio visual techniques

24. For a training program designed to enhance group problem solving skills, which type of seating management is most appropriate?

   a. Classroom style
   b. Chevron style
   c. Circle style
   d. Theater style

25. Tests would likely be used for evaluating the results of training programs when which criterion is utilized?

   a. Reaction
   b. Learning
   c. Behavior
   d. Results

## TRAINING AND DEVELOPMENT
## ANSWERS, RATIONALES, CODING

1. Answer: b. Ensure the selection of trainees is well documented and does not result in adverse impact

   Training is a condition of employment subject to EEO laws. As such, participation opportunities come under the Uniform Guidelines for Employee Selection Procedures (especially when training opens up promotional opportunities). Adverse impact calculations should be made on selection of trainees using the 4/5's rule.

   CODE:    III-A-1

2. Answer: b.    Training department's overhead

   The training department's overhead is an indirect cost spread out over all training programs. All other options are direct costs associated with a single training program.

   CODE:    III-B-3

3. Answer: b.    A needs analysis

   A prerequisite to developing training objectives and a corresponding training program, is a thorough training needs analysis. A needs analysis allows the trainer to specify the objectives so that training programs can be evaluated on how they attain those objectives.

CODE: III-C-1-a

4. Answer: b. Training needs

Determination of training needs is a prerequisite to many other related T&D decisions. For example, training needs must be assessed prior to establishing specific training objectives, program content, method(s) used, or who the trainees should be.

CODE: III-C-1-a

5. Answer: a. Conducting a job/task analysis

A basic way to insure content validity of training programs is to conduct a job/task analysis. The other options are less related to content validity.

CODE: III-C-2

6. Answer: a. Aptitude

Interest tests, such as the Strong-Campbell Interest Blank and the Kuder Preference Record, are helpful in making selection and training decisions. They are also quite useful for counseling purposes. Personality inventories such as the Minnesota Multiphasic Personality Inventory, measure some aspects of one's total personality. Specific abilities tests are used to measure a learned skill or knowledge about a specific occupation.

CODE: III-C-2-g

7. Answer: c. Gestalt learning

The "whole learning" concept is that it is advantageous to provide an overall view of what the trainee will be learning rather than to begin immediately with the specific. Active practice involves actually performing a task as opposed to reading about it. Spaced practice suggests that for some types of training, engaging in practice over a period of time may improve learning. Immediate confirmation is the concept that people learn best when given immediate feedback to their responses.

CODE: III-D-2-b

8. Answer: d. Actively involved in the learning process

It has been suggested that while people retain only a small portion of what they read and hear, they remember up to 90 percent of what they say and do while performing tests. The more senses involved, apparently, the more efficient the retention of information.

CODE: III-D-2-b

9. Answer: b. It rises faster during early stages of learning and more slowly as training continues

A learning curve graphically depicts an individual's learning rate over time. Most individual's learning curves have decreasing returns with the learning rate rapid at first and then slowing down. Often learning curves flatten out or plateau for a period of time. This is usually a temporary condition.

CODE:   III-D-2-b

10.  Answer: a.   Adult

Within the framework of transactional analysis, three separate sources of behavior (ego states) are identified. Attitudes, beliefs and values learned early in our lives from authority figures become part of our parent ego state and influence our current behavior. The emotional side of behavior stems largely from the child ego state. The adult provides us with objectivity. Through this ego state we analyze data and make logical/judgments. Behavioral changes occur through this ego state.

CODE:   III-D-2-b

11.  Answer: a.   Self-nomination

While the cost of assessing every person at particular levels may be prohibitive, reliance upon supervisors to nominate participants also presents difficulties. Employee attributes which are considered important at higher levels may not be valued by supervisors at lower levels in the firm.

CODE:   III-D-2-c

12.  Answer: c.   Evaluative

In **non-listening** the individual totally ignores what is said and, therefore, would not have an opinion about it. **Marginal listening** is related to evaluative in that it occurs on a part-time basis. It does not, however, necessarily involve the premature formation of an opinion about what is being said.

**Projective listening** involves trying to place yourself in the mind of the speaker and thoroughly understand what is being stated before an opinion is formed.

CODE: III-D-2-d

13. Answer: c. The material learned is important to them

Readiness to learn is a function of the importance of the material to be learned. Trainees become much more involved in the process when they appreciate the importance attached to the material to be learned. This is usually accomplished by relating the material back to the trainee's individual situation.

CODE: III-D-2-d

14. Answer: c. Vestibule training

In on-the-job training (OJT), trainees learn while actually performing a job. This is perhaps the most commonly used method and can be very effective if the supervisor-trainer is supportive, provides adequate reinforcement, has the time for training and the pressure to produce is not excessive. Internships, apprenticeships, and coaching are forms of OJT. Vestibule training however, differs in that training is provided in a simulated environment - an area apart from where actual production takes place. The cost of this approach is primary disadvantage.

CODE: III-D-4-h

15. Answer: a. Managerial

    The in-basket training method involves the use of a representative sample of a manager's in-basket over a period of time. The in-basket typically involves a structured array of memos, reports, letters, appointments, and visits associated with a manager's job. The in-basket training method is especially useful to measure and train decision-making skills, organizational and prioritizing abilities, and the ability to grasp interrelationships.

    CODE:      III-D-3-c

16. Answer: c. Sensitivity training

    Organizational development (OD) is designed to increase a firm's effectiveness through planned interventions using behavioral science knowledge. A number of techniques are used in OD, including sensitivity training. This method has the purpose of making individuals aware of themselves and the impact they have on others. Sensitivity training features an unstructured group with no specific agenda. The interaction which takes place in these groups is apparently quite threatening to some people.

    CODE:      III-D-3-d

17. Answer: a. Be modularized and spread out over a period of time

    Too much information, too fast creates information overload and reduces retention of information. To minimize this problem, orientation activities should be broken down into manageable units and spread out over time.

CODE: III-D-3-e

18. Answer: d. Role-play

Role play involves the trainee assuming a role in a mock situation and acting out that role. It is behavioral based allowing the trainee to be given feedback on performance. Discipline and discharge training is ideally suited for role playing.

CODE: III-D-4-d

19. Answer: c. Apprenticeship training

Apprenticeship training involves a cooperative experience between an employer and a union whereby the employee receives on-the-job instruction by a skilled crafts person supplemented by formal classroom instruction outside of work hours. An internship involves classroom and on-the-job instruction but is usually less structured and not directed to specific skills.

CODE: III-D-4-c

20. Answer: a. Expectancy theory

**Reinforcement theory** holds that the <u>consequences</u> of behavior influences that behavior. To be most effective, reinforcement needs to be provided as soon after the desired behavior as possible. **Herzberg's motivation** - hygiene theory focuses on <u>satisfiers</u> or motivators, (such as achievement and responsibility) and <u>dissatisfiers</u>, or hygiene factors which are important in preventing "demotivation" but do not positively motivate performance. Hygiene factors are company policy, working conditions, and pay. **Equity theory** suggests that individuals compare their rewards and the efforts required to attain them with the rewards and efforts of other relevant individuals.

CODE:   III-D-2-b

21. Answer: d.   Behavior modeling

In behavior modeling, trainees observe a supervisor's role play in, for example, disciplining an employee. Since the situations presented are typical of those in the trainee's firm, they are able to relate the behavior on their own jobs. Behavior modeling is a relatively new training approach but it is being used in many well-known large and small organizations.

CODE:   III-D-4-d

22. Answer: c.   Simulation training

Simulation training uses a controlled training situation away from the work site. It provides realistic conditions in an environment where the consequences of errors can be minimized. Business cases and executive games are examples of simulations that are adaptable to planning and conceptual skills. Too often, the concept of simulation only brings to mind skill training such as driver's education or flight training for pilots. The other options, sensitivity training, human relations training and role playing are more appropriate techniques for personal interaction skills training.

CODE: III-D-4-e

23. Answer: c. Programmed instruction

Programmed instruction typically provides a small amount of information to the trainee and then poses a question. If the correct answer is given, the trainee is directed to the next "frame." If the incorrect response is given, the trainee is directed to restudy the information.

CODE: III-D-4-f

24. Answer: c. Circle style

Circle and horseshoe style seating arrangements are especially well suited for highly interactive training such as group problem solving. Classroom, chevron and theater style lend themselves to large group presentations with less trainer-participant interaction.

CODE: III-D-5-c

25. Answer: b. Learning

Training **reaction** to the value of training programs is probably the most widely used criterion for evaluating training programs. In this approach trainees are asked, often using questionnaires, whether the training is useful. **Learning** is what trainees can demonstrate that they know as a result of the training. Using tests, it can be determined if they have learned successfully. When **behavior** is the criterion, the focus is on whether the learning will be applied on the job. Behaviors are most likely to be measured through a performance appraisal system such as BARS. Trainees may believe the training to be useful (reaction), they may even use newly acquired techniques on the job (behavior). However, organizations should be interested in **results**.

CODE:	III-E-3-b

## **COMPENSATION AND BENEFITS- ITEMS**

1. Assuming no willful violation, what is the statute of limitations for recovery of back pay under the Fair Labor Standards Act?

    a.  2 years
    b.  3 years
    c.  4 years
    d.  5 years

2. In order for a postion to qualify under the executive exemption to the Fair Labor Standards Act, the position must

    a.  be considered an officer of the organization.
    b.  have a Bachelor's degree or higher.
    c.  direct the work of at least two other full-time employees.
    d.  spend less than 30% of the time on nonexempt duties.

3. A data entry person earned $8.00 per hour plus a weekly attendance incentive of $20.00. If the employee works 42 hours in a work week, how much total compensation should be paid?

    a.  $356.00
    b.  $364.00
    c.  $365.50
    d.  $372.00

4. Which of the following is NOT included in a party-in-interest as defined by ERISA?

   a. Employee with less than one year of service
   b. Owner of at least 50% of the property of the employer
   c. Trustees, custodians and persons providing services to such a plan
   d. Administrators, fiduciaries and trustees of an employee benefit plan

5. The Employee Retirement Income Security Act of 1974 covers

   a. Employers only
   b. Regular employees only
   c. All employees and employers
   d. All employers with 15 or more employees

6. An expatriate's expenses for home travel are deductible for U.S. tax purposes if the trip is made to

   a. the U.S.
   b. the principal residence in the U.S.
   c. anywhere outside of the country of assignment.
   d. the location of the last employment in the U.S.

7. How do employees tend to perceive the pay of their peers and supervisors when they do not know what the actual pay is?

   a. They overestimate the pay of both their peers and their supervisors.
   b. They underestimate the pay of both their peers and their supervisors.

175

      c.      They underestimate the pay of their peers and overestimate that of their supervisors.
      d.      They overestimate the pay of their peers and underestimate that of their supervisors.

8.    At the beginning of a given year, a Shipping Department has four people, each paid $1,000 per month. In that year, each of these employees receives a pay raise of $100 per month. The raises are given January 1, March 1, July 1 and November 1, respectively. The salary increases increase the payroll cost for the year by

      a.      6.25%.
      b.      7%.
      c.      9%.
      d.      10%.

9.    What would a compa-ratio of 110 indicate?

      a.      Salary range is competitive with market
      b.      Salary range is low in relation to market
      c.      Salary range is high in relation to market
      d.      Average salaries paid are ten percent above the midpoint of the salary range

10.    A two-tiered wage system could be expected to be most effective in

      a.      reducing payroll costs.
      b.      increasing individual motivation.
      c.      relating pay to group performance.
      d.      increasing feelings of external equity.

11. What is the basic requirement for an incentive wage plan?

    a. Union approval
    b. Employee approval
    c. Government approval
    d. A quantifiable volume of work

12. The value of a stock option is directly related to an increase in

    a. earnings per share.
    b. dividends per share.
    c. stock price per share.
    d. gross sales per share.

13. What is a draw, as used for sales representatives?

    a. Money that is to be used to pay for traveling expenses
    b. Money that is paid on a regular basis in addition to commissions
    c. Money that is paid on a regular basis but that must be earned from commissions or paid back
    d. Money that is paid on a regular basis to be applied against commissions but not paid back if unearned

14. What pay plan is most likely to motivate a field salesperson?

    a. Base salary only
    b. Base salary plus profit sharing
    c. Base salary plus group incentive
    d. Base salary plus individual incentive

15. For which of the following types of employees are maturity curves most used as a basis of compensation?

   a. Executives
   b. Management trainees
   c. Professional personnel
   d. Long service nonexempt employees

16. An organization which desires to use a job analysis method which allows for a quick response rate and gathering of data on a large number of jobs, should use which method of job analysis?

   a. Observation
   b. Interview
   c. Questionnaire
   d. Functional Job Analysis

17. Under the factor comparison system, jobs are evaluated through the use of

   a. predetermined wage classes.
   b. a company conversion table.
   c. a scale developed from key jobs.
   d. market pricing criteria only.

18. A salary survey shows the following data:

   | Organization | Number Incumbents | Average Salary |
   |---|---|---|
   | A | 15 | $ 700 |
   | B | 10 | 700 |
   | C | 25 | 700 |
   | D | 50 | 800 |

How does the weighted average salary compare to the unweighted average salary?

a. It is $50 lower
b. It is $25 lower
c. It is $25 higher
d. It is $50 higher

19. In the majority of companies using rate ranges, where is the market value of a job considered to be?

a. The minimum
b. The maximum
c. The midpoint
d. The 75th percentile

20. In translating the results of a salary survey into actual wage rates, what statistical technique would be most appropriate to use?

a. Least-squares method
b. Dispersion method
c. Correlation method
d. Expected variance method

21. After implementing a new job evaluation plan, it is best to deal with red circle rates by

a. reducing their salary to the new maximum for their respective job grade.
b. allowing their base rate to increase as all others do in the same job grade.

c. reducing the salary to the minimum of the range and providing the employee the amount of the decrease in the form of a bonus.
d. freezing their salary until job grade maximum increases to catch up with the red circle rate.

22. Educational assistance plans most often reimburse the employee on

   a. the type of school attended.
   b. the type of position an employee occupies.
   c. successful course completion.
   d. promotion potential.

23. Greater flexibility for employees can be built into a vacation leave program by

   a. providing more vacation time.
   b. reducing the advance notice period.
   c. allowing a carry-over of unused leave.
   d. having supervisors assign leave time.

24. Which of the following would least likely occur with the implementation of a cafeteria-style benefits program?

   a. Reduced turnover
   b. Less wasted or unused benefits
   c. Reduced administrative costs
   d. Increased employee understanding of benefits costs

25. A large employer has found that its past total insurance claims have been stable. A few very large claims have been paid and

a large sum has been paid for premium taxes on the insurance contract. The employer's best option is to seriously consider

a. obtaining insurance through another carrier.
b. a minimum premium plan to control liability and save costs.
c. retaining the current insurance contract due to large claims.
d. self-insurance due to the stability of the amount of total claims.

# COMPENSATION AND BENEFITS
# ANSWERS, RATIONALES, CODING

1. Answer: a.   2 years

    The FLSA has a two year statute of limitations for recovery of back pay. In cases of a willful or intentional violation, a three year statute of limitations is available. Records should be kept this three year period unless state law impores a more sturgent standard.

    CODE:   IV-A-2

2. Answer: c.   Direct the work of at least two other full-time employees

    Under the FLSA, an executive must have as a primary duty management and direct 2 or more full-time employees, routinely exercise discretion, have authority to hire or fire, spend less than 20% of their time on nonexempt work and be paid a salary of $155 per week or more.

    CODE:   IV-A-2-a

3. Answer: c.   $365.50

    In calculating overtime, incentive/bonus money is figured in the base rate to determine the overtime rate (1.5 times base). Calculation is 40 hours x $8/hr = $320 for regular base rate. Overtime rate is $320 plus $20 = $340 ($8.50/hr) x 1.5 or $12.75/hr. Total compensation is $320 base rate plus $20 bonus plus $25.50 (2 hrs x $12.75) overtime for $365.50.

CODE: IV-A-2-b

4. Answer: a. Employees with less than one year of service

Under ERISA a party-in-interest include all individuals who come under or have impact on a qualified plan. Owners, trustees, administrators, etc., all are considered a party-in-interest. Until an individual becomes a participant in a plan, they are not considered a party-in-interest.

5. Answer: b. Regular employees only

ERISA when passed in 1974 was designed to regulate private pension plans to assure that participants would receive retirement income when they retire. As such, it was applicable to regular employees only.

CODE: IV-A-9

6. Answer: b. The principal residence in the U.S.

The Internal Revenue Service will allow home travel expenses to be deductible from taxes only if it were to the expatriates principal residence within the United States. Other locations are not tax deductible.

CODE: IV-B-2

183

7. Answer: d. They overestimate the pay of their peers and underestimate that of their supervisors

Research (Lawler, 1972; Milkovich and Anderson, 1972) indicates employees overestimate the pay of their peers and underestimate the pay of supervisors. The greater the overestimation the greater the level of dissatisfaction with pay. As a result of this research, more organizations are moving away from pay secrecy to more open pay systems.

CODE:   IV-B-3-a

8. Answer: a.   6.25%

Count up the remaining months of the increase for January (12), March (10), July (6), and November (2) (equals 30 months at $100 month). Divide $3,000 by the total starting payroll costs $48,000. The increase is 6.25%.

CODE:   IV-D-3-d

9. Answer: d. Average salaries paid are ten percent above the midpoint of the salary range

A coma-ratio is a pay level divided by the midpoint of the pay range. In this case a compa-ratio of 110 indicates the person is ten percent above the midpoint (100).

CODE:   IV-D-4

10. Answer: a. Reducing payroll costs

A two-tiered wage system is one where new employees receive lower wages than existing employees performing similar work. This form of compensation was used in the 1980's in unionized environments to reduce labor costs providing job security for existing employees. This system works best where the employer is paying more than what is necessary to attract and retain employees.

CODE: IV-E

11. Answer: d. A quantifiable volume of work

Incentive systems must be directly tied to performance to be effective. Employees must see a direct relationship between their efforts and their rewards. Additionally employees must see their rewards as equitable and desirable.

CODE: IV-E-3

12. Answer: c. Stock price per share

A stock option gives an employee the right to buy stock in a company usually at an advantageous price. That advantageous price is usually a fixed price available for a fixed period of time which is discounted from the stocks price per share on the market.

CODE: IV-E-3-e

13. Answer: c.   Money that is paid on a regular basis, but that must be earned from commissions or paid back

   A draw is an amount advanced and repaid from future commissions. A draw system allows a salesperson to even out compensation between high and low sales periods. A risk to employers is that future commission may not be large enough to cover the draw.

   CODE:    IV-E-4-b

14. Answer: d.   Base salary plus individual incentive

   Sales persons are most likely motivated by individual incentives tied to volume of sales. Although group incentives, including profit sharing have some motivational impact, the impact is less than for individual incentives such as commissions or bonus programs.

   CODE:    IV-E-4-b

15. Answer: c.   Professional personnel

   Maturity curves are a compensation plan which depicts the relationship between experience in a career field and pay level. They are most appropriate to professionals in science, engineering, architecture and related fields.

   CODE:    IV-E-4-c

16. Answer: c. Questionnaire

   Questionnaires, as a means of gathering job analysis data, provide the most efficient use of resources when data must be collected on many jobs. Questionnaires are self-administered allowing them to be given to many participants at once. They may be open-ended allowing great flexibility or highly structured to fit compensation or validation needs. Observation is very time consuming especially for long cycle jobs. Likewise, individual interviews require quite a bit of time. Functional Job Analysis, used by the Federal government, is highly structured and requires extensive resources.

   CODE: IV-F-1-c

17. Answer: c. A scale developed from key jobs

   Factor comparison job evaluation plans are a combination of ranking and point factor job evaluation plans. Benchmarks of key jobs are selected. These are jobs which have been stable over time and most people will relate with. Factors are ranked for each benchmarked job and assigned a score reflecting their ranking. The process is continued for all compensable factors, one at a time. The scores are totaled for each job, resulting in a discrete job ranking.

   CODE: IV-G-4

18. Answer: c.   It is $25 higher

    The unweighted average salary is 700 + 700 + 700 + 800(2,900) divided by 4 = $725. The weighted average salary is calculated as follows:

    | 15 x 700 | = 10,500 |
    | 10 x 700 | =  7,000 |
    | 25 x 700 | = 17,500 |
    | 50 x 800 | = 40,000 |
    | 100 | 75,000 divided by 100 = $750 |

    CODE:      IV-H-1

19. Answer: c.   The midpoint

    Most traditional job evaluation plans establish the midpoint of the salary range to equal average salaries paid in the marketplace. The relationship to the midpoint then becomes an important concept in making individual pay determinations. A compa-ratio becomes a useful number in expressing relationship to the midpoint.

    CODE:      IV-H-1-a

20. Answer: a.   Least squares method

    The least squares method of regression analysis is a technique for fitting a line to data plotted on a graph to determine the degree of correlation (or significance) between two variables. In building a salary structure, the plotted line is referred to as the trend line and salary grades are built upon it.

    CODE:      IV-H-1-a

21. Answer: d.   Freezing their salary until job grade maximum increases catch up with the red circle rate

A red circle rate is where the incumbent is paid above the rate range maximum for the job. Red circle rates come about either through the administration of a new job evaluation plan or whereby an employee may take a demotion. The standard practice for handling red circle rates is to freeze the incumbent's salary until such time as the range catches up to the rate.

CODE:   IV-H-2

22. Answer: c.   Successful course completion

Most educational assistance plans reimburse after successful completion of the course. Successful completion is usually defined as a passing grade of C or better for undergraduate courses and a grade of B or better for graduate courses.

CODE:   IV-I

23. Answer: c.   Allowing a carry-over of unused leave

Accrual of vacation leave along with year end carry-over allows employees to accumulate vacation leave for special occasions. If the amount of carryover is great, it can create a cash flow problem for employers when taken or paid out upon termination.

CODE:   IV-I-5-a

24. Answer: c. Reduced administrative costs

Cafeteria-style benefit plans allow employees some degree of freedom of selection in the type of benefits for which they may enroll. These plans allow the employee to tailor the benefit package to their particular life situation thereby providing a more efficient utilization of benefits. The downside of such plans are increased record keeping and administration and the potential for "adverse selection."

CODE: IV-I-7

25. Answer: b. A minimum premium plan to control liability and save costs

Option b. is the best answer from two points of view. First is the avoidance of risk. A minimum premium plan will have less risk from large claims to the company than going to a totally self-funded plan. Second is the cost reduction to the company. Costs will be reduced due to fewer dollars paid for premium tax and investment income from reserves that would have been paid to the insurance company under a fully insured approach. Since it is a large company with stable claims, it can also project its cost and budget for them.

CODE: IV-J-7

## EMPLOYEE AND LABOR RELATIONS - ITEMS

1. Under the Worker Adjustment and Retraining Notification Act (1988), if a covered employer is to close a plant, it must provide _____ days notice to the employees' representative.

    a. 30
    b. 60
    c. 90
    d. 120

2. What restriction is placed on NLRB certification of a unit of security guards?

    a. The same restrictions as in units of other employees
    b. The union seeking certification must represent only guards
    c. The expiration date of the guards contract cannot coincide with that of the plant union
    d. The union must include all plant employees

3. In order for a union to prevail during a representation election, it must

    a. win a majority of the votes cast in an election.
    b. win 51% of the votes of those eligible to vote in the election.
    c. win two-thirds of the votes cast in the election.
    d. win 30% of the votes cast.

4. Which of the following may legally be stated in an organization's employee relations policy?

   a. Increase pay for remaining non-union
   b. Plant closure if unionized
   c. Organizational opposition to unions
   d. Endorsement of a specific union

5. During a unionization drive, which of the following may a supervisor legally do?

   a. Visit the homes of employees for the purpose of urging them to reject the union
   b. Inform the employees that he/she believes the international union may attempt to control the local membership
   c. Make speeches to massed assemblies of employees on company time within a 24 hour period of time before the election
   d. Speak to employees one-on-one in the office of the management official and urge them to vote against the union

6. During a grievance hearing involving discipline, the union contends the company has not applied discipline in this case as it has in others involving very similar circumstances. They ask to see the discipline records of two other employees to back up this contention. Which of the following is the appropriate company response?

   a. Provide the discipline records
   b. Provide the discipline records only if the two employees authorize the release of records

c. Inform the union to go to court to subpoena the records
d. Reject the unions request

7. When a union is attempting to organize within a company, which of the following is a permissible management statement?

a. "If you join the union, we may have to cut your wages."
b. "If the union organizes here, we may have to shut down."
c. "If a union organizes here, you are going to have to foot the bill by paying union dues."
d. "If the union gets turned down, we may all get a raise."

8. The company and union are preparing to begin negotiations at a local mote. The company president instructs the HR manager to pick up all motel costs including meals and transportation for both sides. What should the HR manager do?

a. Pick up the entire bill
b. Pick up meal expenses only
c. Pick up motel room expenses only
d. Advise the president that such action is unlawful

9. For many years, employees at a certain company took two daily 10-minute coffee breaks. After being organized, the company received a request for two 15-minute coffee breaks. The company should:

   a. Discontinue its practice
   b. Continue its practice and negotiate
   c. Discontinue its practice and negotiate
   d. Continue the practice but refuse to negotiate

10. Good faith bargaining requires that both labor and management

    a. reach agreement on the mandatory items under negotiation.
    b. meet and discuss those mandatory items brought up by the other side.
    c. fairly represent themselves by not making inflammatory statements about the other side.
    d. reach agreement on all mandatory and permissive items brought up by the other side.

11. During negotiations the union and company were discussing wage increases for production operators. The company claimed that granting a wage increase would give the operators more money than the supervisors were making. The union requested the salary schedules for supervisors. What is the company required to do?

    a. Refuse the request
    b. Provide the supervisors salary schedule to the union

c. Refuse the request, but give the information to a mediator
d. Ignore the request

12. When a mediator is called in to resolve a collective bargaining impasse, the mediator

    a. may order the parties back to the bargaining table to break the impasse.
    b. makes a decision which is binding upon both parties.
    c. has authority to go to court to break the impasse.
    d. functions only to bring the parties together to find common ground to break the impasse.

13. Which of the following approaches will most effectively minimize employee relations difficulties?

    a. Install a suggestion system
    b. Increase the amount of supervision provided employees
    c. Maintain an open line of direct and factual communication with employees
    d. Implement a quality control program

14. An effective labor relations program will teach first-line supervisors to view grievances as:

    a. Win-lose situations
    b. Policy making sessions
    c. Problem solving mechanisms
    d. Compromises of company policy

15. In an arbitration proceeding, it is agreed by all parties that the action complained about is a very slight departure from what is required in the labor contract. In such a case, the arbitrator is most likely to present the rule of

    a. reason.
    b. parole evidence.
    c. de minimis.
    d. management by exception.

16. When a grievance goes to final and binding arbitration, arbitrators base their decisions on

    a. their interpretation of the language of the labor agreement.
    b. the intent of the parties when the labor agreement was negotiated
    c. past arbitrations dealing with the same issue in different organizations.
    d. the position of the National Labor Relations Board on the issue.

17. Which of the following work rule violations is generally dealt with more severely when employees are first offenders?

    a. Negligence
    b. Insubordination
    c. Absenteeism and tardiness
    d. Performance of personal work on company time

18. The primary test to determine the reasonableness of a work rule is whether or not the

   a. union has requested a change in the rule or its elimination.
   b. rule furthers a strict disciplinary approach to managing the workforce.
   c. employees agree that the rule is necessary if the plant is to operate efficiently.
   d. rule is reasonably related to a legitimate business reason.

19. A manager summons a unionized employee to the managers office to be interviewed about a work rule violation. The employee demands a union representative be present. Which of the following responses should the manager give?

   a. The meeting will be conducted without the union representative present, because it is a management's right to discipline.
   b. No grievance has been filed so there is no entitlement to union representation.
   c. A union representative is only permitted if the contract provides for union representation at discipline meetings.
   d. A union representative may be present for investigative meetings which lead to discipline if requested by the employee.

20. If an HR manager notices the posting of a number of pin-ups--fold-outs of scantily clothed females--out on the shop floor, the HR manager should have the posters removed based upon which theory of sexual harassment?

    a. Employment consequence
    b. Employment conditions
    c. Vicarious liability
    d. Hostile environment

21. When significant aspects of performance are not measured by the appraisal form, this is called:

    a. Criterion contamination
    b. Criterion deficiency
    c. Rater bias error
    d. Contrast error

22. If a supervisor gives an employee a very high rating on "quality of work" and allows that rating to influence the rating on "quantity of work," the supervisor is guilty of:

    a. Leniency error
    b. Central tendency error
    c. Raterbias error
    d. Halo/horned error

23. In performance appraisal systems, central tendency is the most common error found in using:

    a. Essays
    b. Ranking

c. Critical incidents
d. Graphic rating scales

24. Multisource assessments (360 degrees appraisals) are most relevant and useful for:

   a. Retention decisions
   b. Developmental purposes
   c. Merit pay decisions
   d. Candidates for international assignments

25. What is the most prevalent problem associated with the use of employees attitude surveys?

   a. Surveys are administered in-house
   b. Employees are informed of survey results
   c. Survey results are not responded to by management
   d. Surveys are administered prior to management perceiving a problem

## EMPLOYEE AND LABOR RELATIONS
## ANSWERS, RATIONALES, CODING

1. Answer: b.   60

    If an employer has 100 or more employees and it anticipates a plant closing affecting 50 or more employees or a mass lay-off affecting 33% of employees or 50 workers, it must provide the employees' representative 60 days written notice. If the employees have no representative, the employer must notify each affected employee prior to 60 days before such action.

    CODE:      V-A-8

2. Answer: b.   The union seeking certification must represent only guards

    Due to divided loyalties and a conflict of interest, the NLRB has determined that plant guards must be in a separate union from other plant employees. During a strike situation, guards are responsible for protecting company property. Separating the guards into a different bargaining unit helps alleviate this problem.

    CODE:      V-B-3-b

3. Answer: a.   Win a majority of the votes cast in an election

    Much like political elections in the U.S., the NLRB requires that a union win a majority of the votes cast during a representation election in order to certify the union. It is important, therefore, that all eligible employees participate in the voting so that a small minority doesn't determine the fate of many.

CODE: V-B-4

4. Answer: c. Organizational opposition to unions

An organization can legally state their opposition to the unionization of employees. A pay increase for remaining non-union is a promise which constitutes an unfair labor practice. Likewise, a plant closure is a threat and also an unfair labor practice if done only to avoid the union. Endorsement of a specific union is also an unfair labor practice which could be construed as setting up a "company union."

CODE: V-C-2

5. Answer: b. Inform the employees that he/she believes the international union may attempt to control local membership

Employers are free to educate employees as long as they don't spy, threaten, coerce or promise. Employers may make speeches to employees (captive audiences) but not within 24 hours of an election. Visiting the homes of employees and one-on-one discussions in management offices are clearly out of bounds.

CODE: V-C-2

203

6. Answer: a. Provide the discipline records

In general, an employer is responsible for furnishing information to the union in order for the union to discharge its contract negotiations and administration responsibilities. The information must be directly relevant to the issue at hand. In this instance, the union is seeking discipline records in "similar" circumstances, so the unions request is appropriate. Failure to provide the information could constitute an unfair labor practice.

CODE:    V-C-2

7. Answer: c. "If a union organizes here, you are going to have to foot the bill by paying union dues"

Management may legitimately educate employees regarding unions as long as it does not threaten, promise or coerce employees. During an organizing campaign the TIPS rule should be kept in mind. It is an unfair labor practice for an employer to Threaten, Interrogate, Promise, or Spy on employees.

CODE:    V-C-2

8. Answer: d. Advise the president that such action is unlawful

It is an unfair labor practice for an employer to dominate or interfere with the formation and administration of any labor organization or contribute financial support to it. In this situation, the only permissible action on the part of the employer would be to share equally with the union, the total costs of the negotiation facility.

CODE: V-C-3-a

9. Answer: b. Continue its practice and negotiate

Coffee breaks are a mandatory subject for negotiation. However, the employer is under no obligation to change past practice until the item has been negotiated. Unions oftentimes attempt to change past practice outside of the bargaining environment. The employer's best strategy is to deal with the issue through the formalized structure of collective bargaining.

CODE: V-E-1-b

10. Answer: b. Meet and discuss those mandatory items brought up by the other side

Good faith bargaining does not require either side to agree to anything. The only requirement is that they meet and discuss the mandatory issues brought up by the other side. Good faith is measured by the totality of the conduct of the party.

CODE: V-E-3

11. Answer: b. Provide the supervisors salary schedule to the union

Management has a duty to provide relevant information to a union for purposes of collective bargaining. Determining what is relevant is oftentimes problematic. If a rationale for not granting a pay increase involves a pay compression problem with supervisors, the union is entitled to such information. If management did not use this rationale, it would be under no obligation to provide the supervisor's salary schedule.

CODE:  V-E-3-a

12. Answer: d.  Functions only to bring the parties together to find common ground to break the impasse

A mediator is a neutral third party whose function it is to keep the parties talking. They have no formal power other than that of persuasion. They may not make orders, binding decisions or go to court to enforce their authority.

CODE:  V-E-9

13. Answer: c.  Maintain an open line of direct and factual communication with employees

Research has consistently shown that many employees are uninformed and misinformed in most organizations. The most effective employee relations initiative of the options listed is in communication. First line supervisors serve the key role in keeping the lines of communication both open and factual.

CODE:  V-F-4

14. Answer: c.  Problem solving mechanisms

An effective labor relations program focuses on teaching supervisors how to resolve grievances at the lowest level process. Grievances should be viewed as problems which should be resolved through the bounds of the labor agreement. Point scoring, win-lose situations, abdication of management rights are all dysfunctional approaches to grievance handling.

CODE:    V-F-2

15.  Answer: c.   De minimis

Minor violations of a collective bargaining agreement are generally not accorded much weight by arbitrators. These "de minimis" violations, although technically wrong, do not generally result in substantial harm to either party. Only when a pattern of such "de minimis" violations arise will an arbitrator address a remedy in an award.

CODE:    V-F-3-c

16.  Answer: a.   Their interpretation of the language of the labor agreement

Arbitrators are bound by "the four corners of the document" meaning they must interpret the specific language of the labor agreement. The labor agreement becomes controlling and the arbitration award is issued addressing the specific issue in question, under the specific clause of the labor agreement, in a specific organizational setting. As long as arbitrators act within the slope and bounds of their authority their decisions can not be successfully appealed to the judicial system.

CODE:    V-F-3-e

17. Answer: b.   Insubordination

    Insubordination implies a knowing act on the part of the employee to refuse a reasonable order or direction from an authorized supervisor. It is the hallmark of order and efficiency in the workplace and is accorded more weight than the other work rule violations listed.

    CODE:   V-H-1-a

18. Answer: d.   Rule is reasonably related to a legitimate business reason

    Work rules cannot be arbitrary and capricious. They must relate to a legitimate business reason in order to be upheld.

    CODE:   V-H-1-a

19. Answer: d.   A union representative may be present for investigative meetings which lead to discipline if requested by the employee

    Under the Weingarten decision (NLRB v. Weingarten, Inc. 420 U.S. 262, 1974), the U.S. Supreme Court ruled that union representation must be given to an employee when the employee requests representation and the employee reasonably believes the investigation will result in disciplinary action.

    CODE:   V-H-1-d

20. Answer: d. Hostile environment

The posting of pin-ups is an example of a hostile environment theory of sexual harassment. Under this theory, sexual harassment is often not directed at one person but creates an environment which interferes with work performance. The use of sexually suggestive jokes can also be an example of the hostile environment theory. There are no employment conditions or consequences from the pin-up.

CODE: V-H-3-a

21. Answer: b. Criterion deficiency

**Criterion deficiency** occurs when significant aspects of job performance are not being captured by the appraisal instrument. **Criterion contamination** occurs when the appraisal instrument captures non-relevant factors to performance. **Rater bias** is the prejudice of the rater which influences ratings. **Contrast error** is rating one employee higher or lower not based upon objective performance but based upon how they compare to another employee.

CODE: V-J-2-a

22. Answer: d. Halo/horned error

Allowing the rating of one area of performance to influence the rating of another area of performance is a criterion contamination problem frequently referred to as the halo/horned effect. If the influence is positive, it is the halo effect. If the influence is negative, it is the horned effect. **Leniency** is rating all employees very high. Its opposite is strictness or rating all employees very low.  **Central tendency** involves rating persons in a narrow band in the middle of a rating scale.  **Rater bias** occurs when a rater's values or prejudices distorts the ratings.

CODE:    V-J-2-b

23.   Answer: d.    Graphic rating scales

Central tendency is a common problem associated with a graphic rating scale performance appraisal.  The rater evaluates all employees as average or in the mid-range of the scale.  In effect, the rater is not making any judgments.

CODE:    V-J-4-a

24.   Answer: b.    Developmental purposes

Multisource assessments are also referred to as 360 degree feedback, full circle feedback and multirater assessment.  First, critical competencies, behaviors or values are identified.  Then managers are evaluated on these skill sets by having employees directly reporting to the person, internal and external customers, peers or co-workers, or superiors complete a confidential survey about the persons ability.  The summarized data is shared with the manager for developmental purposes.  Multisource assessments are popular in team environments.

CODE:    V-J-7

25. Answer: c. Survey results are not responded to by management

Administering an attitude survey to employees implies that the results will be followed-up by management. If employees are to voluntarily participate in such surveys, they must believe that the feedback will result in change. Research has indicated that failure to share results and to respond to problems significantly reduces participation in subsequent surveys.

CODE: V-K-3-b

## HEALTH, SAFETY AND SECURITY - ITEMS

1. The least serious OSHA violation is:

    a. other-than-serious
    b. de minimis
    c. serious
    d. willful and repeated

2. Under the Drug Free Workplace Act (1988), an employer with government contracts over $25,000 must do all of the following EXCEPT:

    a. Terminate employees for off-time job drug usage
    b. Inform employees of drug-free requirements
    c. Outline actions to be taken
    d. Establish awareness programs and supervisory training

3. Which of the following factors is the most critical to employee acceptance of an employee assistance program?

    a. Cost
    b. Qualifications of counselors
    c. Sources of referral
    d. Confidentiality

4. Which type of data is generally unavailable to a HR manager in evaluating the effectiveness of an external Employee Assistance Program?

    a. Initial diagnosis category
    b. Referral source

c. Vitalization percent
d. Treatment outcome

5. A supervisor who has an employee with a suspected alcohol problem impacting performance should

   a. confront the employee immediately about the alcohol problem.
   b. diagnose the employee's problem before trying to counsel him/her.
   c. document the situation before discussing the decreased performance with the employee.
   d. never expect the employee to return to his/her previous performance level.

6. Employers under the OSHA Bloodborne Pathogens standard must:

   a. Provide free hepatitis B vaccinations to all employees
   b. Establish a written exposure control plan
   c. Communicate an employee's bloodborne infection status to co-workers upon request
   d. Conduct regular blood tests on all employees

7. According to research, the most critical factors to accident prevention are:

   a. Work rules and discipline
   b. Safety posters and ergonomics
   c. Pay and reward systems
   d. Protective equipment and safety training

8. An HR manager, upon learning of a high incidence of repetitive motion disorders or carpel tunnel syndrome among data entry personnel would most likely employ the services of a(n):

    a. Industrial engineer
    b. Ergonomist
    c. Industrial hygienist
    d. Occupational therapist

9. The most fundamental step to dealing with the issue of violence in the workplace is for an HR manager to establish:

    a. A discipline system to deal with potentially violent employees
    b. A selection system which screens out potentially violent applicants
    c. A violence response team
    d. Training for supervisors in identifying potentially violent employees

10. A polygraph examination may be used to investigate allegations of employee theft

    a. only in the pharmaceutical manufacturing industry.
    b. when an experienced polygraph examiner is used.
    c. when the results are not the sole criteria of an employment decision.
    d. when adverse impact analysis is used in conjunction with the polygraph examination.

## HEALTH, SAFETY AND SECURITY
## ANSWERS, RATIONALES, CODING

1. Answer: b.  de minimis

   OSHA categorizes violations in the following manner--de minimis, other-than-serious, serious, willful and repeated, and imminent danger. A de minimis violation does not have a direct and immediate relationship to employees' health and safety. An other-than-serious violation could have an impact on employees' health and safety, but would not cause death or serious harm and the employer should know the condition. Willful and repeated violations are when the employer has previously been cited by OSHA for the same condition.

   CODE:     VI-A-1-c

2. Answer: a.  Terminate employees for off-time job drug usage

   The Drug Free Workplace Act deals with only on-the-job drug use. Many employers refer employees with drug abuse problems to Employee Assistance Programs or other professional treatment sources.

   CODE:     VI-A-3-a

3. Answer: d.  Confidentiality

   Research has indicated that when employees have personal problems, their primary concern is that they can receive help on a confidential basis from an employee assistance plan.

Although the other options are all factors, confidentiality is the most critical to employee acceptance.

CODE: VI-B-2-e

4. Answer: d. Treatment outcome

Most Employee Assistance Programs provide periodic reports to employers outlining activity in the program. In order to protect employee confidentiality, information is compiled in such a way to guarantee enormity. Treatment outcome is almost never reported back to the employer. The other information--initial diagnosis category, referral source and utilization is typically found in EAP provider reports.

CODE: VI-B-2-f

5. Answer: c. Document the situation before discussing the decreased performance with the employee

In general, supervisors are ill equipped to handle alcohol related problems in the workplace. They should not confront nor counsel employee's suffering from alcoholism. They deal with the situation as a performance problem and refer the employee to professional help.

CODE: VI-B-5

216

6.  Answer:  b.  Establish a written exposure control plan

The OSHA Bloodborne Pathogens Standard requires employers that are subject to OSHA and have <u>any</u> employees who have on-the-job exposure to blood or other bodily fluids must take the following steps:

1.  Establish a written exposure control plan
2.  Observe universal precautions
3.  Identify and adopt engineering and work practice controls
4.  Provide personal protective equipment
5.  Develop housekeeping, waste management and laundry standards
6.  Make available free hepatitis B vaccinations to those employees <u>with</u> occupational exposure
7.  Establish post-exposure evaluation
8.  Communicate hazards to employees
9.  Maintain specific recordkeeping

CODE:   VI-B-6-d

7.  Answer:  d.  Protective equipment and safety training

A number of research studies have shown that providing employees personal safety protective equipment and safety training has the greatest impact on accident prevention. The other factors, although important to an accident prevention program, are less important than protective equipment and training.

CODE:   VI-C-3-e

217

8.  Answer: b.   Ergonomist

    An ergonomist is a professional who deals in the science of ergonomics -- the field of making jobs, facilities, equipment and furnishings fit people. The ergonomist studies the physiological, psychological and engineering design aspects of a job. Human factors engineering is a specialty area within ergonomics. The **industrial engineer** looks only at the engineering design aspects of the job. The **industrial hygienist** looks at environmental factors. An **occupational therapist** works with employees in rehabilitation after a repetitive motion disorder injury.

    CODE:      VI-C-5

9.  Answer: b.   A selection system which screens out potentially violent applicants

    "An ounce of prevention is worth a pound of cure" according to Benjamin Franklin. A selection system designed to assess risk factors and screen out those applicants represents the best starting point. The other options although important in a threat of violence program, should be preceded by an effective selection system. Such system may include psychological testing, risk assessment interviewing, and reference checking.

    CODE:      VI-D-1-g

10. Answer: c. When the results are not the sole criteria of an employment decision

According to the Employee Polygraph Protection Act (1988) a polygraph may be used to investigate employee theft when the employee had access to property which is the subject of the investigation and when the employer had "reasonable suspicion" that the employee was involved in the incident. The results of a polygraph examination may not stand alone.

CODE: VI-D-5-a

# FREQUENTLY ASKED QUESTIONS

# FREQUENTLY ASKED QUESTIONS

The following questions are among those most frequently asked about the HRCI and its certification program. The questions have been answered and are grouped into the following six areas:

>Application for Examination
>Preparation for Examination
>HR Body of Knowledge
>The Certification Examination
>Examination Administration
>Recertification

Application for Examination

**Q. -** **Why would my HRCI Certification Examination Application be returned or rejected?**

A. - The most common reasons for Certification Examination Applications being returned are:
- No signature on the form
- Not including a check or credit card number and expiration date with the application
- Sending a personal check for the fee rather than a money order, cashier's check or organizational check
- Leaving important parts of the form blank
- Not including the Professional Employment Experience Form
- Submitting a faxed or photo-copied application.

The most common reasons for rejecting an application are:
- Receiving the application after the Extended Application Receipt Deadline
- Not possessing the required amount of exempt-level HR experience for the requested examination

Q. - Are examination fees discounted for SHRM members?

A. - Yes. HRCI is a separate organization from SHRM. However, SHRM founded HRCI and for many years, financed its operations. Today, HRCI is self-supporting. The discounted fee for SHRM members is a professional courtesy to SHRM in appreciation of those earlier years of support.

Q. - Why does HRCI require exempt-level HR experience to meet the eligibility requirements to sit for the examination?

A. - Because HRCI grants **professional** certification in the human resource management field. Certification is not granted for paraprofessional or other non exempt experience. One must possess an Executive, Administrative, or Professional exemption under the Fair Labor Standards Act for either the PHR or SPHR examination.

Q. - I qualify for the SPHR exam but am afraid I might not pass it. Should I take the PHR exam instead?

A.. - If you just barely meet the eligibility requirements for the SPHR exam and you haven't had education or experience in each of the six functional areas of the examination, it might be prudent to sit for the PHR exam. However, if you have had a broad range of experience/education and exceed the eligibility requirements it might be best to sit for the SPHR. The general rule of thumb is to sit for the examination for which you qualify and feel most comfortable.

Preparation for Examination

Q. - **What is the best way to prepare?**

A. - There is no single best way to prepare. A lot depends on your prior education and background in the HR field. A lot depends on your learning style. A lot depends on your life style. You should select a preparation method which best matches each of these areas. It may be a high flexible approach such as individual self-study, or a moderately structured approach such as a course or the SHRM Learning System. Remember you can't teach to the HRCI examinations; you have to master the HRCI outline and be able to apply it.

Q. - **Does HRCI recommend learning resources?**

A. - HRCI does not endorse any one learning resource as being qualitatively better than another. But at the same time, those resources based upon the HRCI Content Outline are better focused to help prepare candidates.

Q. - **How do I know if I am ready to sit for the examination?**

A. - Look at the HRCI Content Outline. If you can honestly say you are comfortable with each of the topic areas covered on the outline, you are probably in pretty good shape to sit for the examination. It is also a good idea to use a self-assessment and see how you do on the Practice Examination in this guide.

## HR Body of Knowledge

**Q. -** **Why is the HRCI Content Outline so important?**

A. - Because it serves as a blue print for the HRCI examinations. The weightings on the outline correspond to the weightings of the examination. Candidates will only be tested on subject matter included in the outline.

**Q. -** **How often does HRCI revise its content outline?**

A.- A major revision occurs every five years as a result of the HRCI Codification Process Practitioner Survey. Minor revisions occur yearly as a result of expert or literature reviews. Always make sure you are using the current year's HRCI outline to prepare.

## The Certification Examination

**Q. -** **Where do the examination questions come from?**

A. - They are written by certified HR professionals. They are not written by academics or professional test developers. Because they are developed by certified HR practitioners, the questions tend to be very practical and applied. HRCI examination scores correlate with years of experience and with education.

**Q. -** **How reliable are the examinations?**

A. - Very reliable. If you do not pass an examination and decide to retake it without extensive preparation or additional experience, your results will be similar to the first examination.

**Q. -** **Are HRCI examinations validated?**

A. - Yes. HRCI examinations are content validated. The blue print for HRCI examinations come from the HRCI Content Outline. That outline is the result of the HRCI Codification Process which is much like a job analysis for the entire HR field. Only questions which correspond to the content outline are utilized on the examination forms. Contributing further to this content validation model is the fact that HRCI uses only certified HR professionals to write items, to review items, to review test forms and to analyze the performance of examinations. The HRCI content validation model conforms with the highest standards in the certification testing field.

Q. - What is the best predictor of success on the examination?

A. - Education and experience in the HR field is the best predictor of success on the HRCI examinations.

Q. - Is the examination administered on one test date easier or more difficult than one used on another test date?

A. - HRCI uses a statistical procedure called equating to correct for any differences in difficulty between different forms of the same test. This equating process results in a scaled score rather than a raw score.

Q. - What is the difference between a raw score and a scaled score?

A. - A raw score is the actual number of items answered correctly on the examination. A scaled score, is a score placed on a uniform scale which reflects differences in difficulty levels of different forms of the same examination. A scaled score ensures that every examinee, no matter when they took the examination, must achieve the same uniform standard. A passing score on an HRCI examination is a scaled score of 500. This process ensures consistency and fairness between examination forms.

**Q. -** **Are certain functional areas of the examination more difficult than others?**

**A. -** The answer is based upon the education and experience you bring to the examination. For instance, if you have never worked in a unionized environment one would assume that the employee and labor relations questions on the examination would be more difficult for you. Its really an individual matter. Each of the six functional areas of the examinations have questions with a fairly broad range of difficulty levels.

**Q. -** **Why are PHR and SPHR examinations weighted differently?**

**A. -** The PHR and SPHR exams differ in terms of focus and cognitive level of questions. The PHR exam questions tend to be at the operational/technical level, whereas the SPHR questions tend to be at the strategic and/or policy level. Therefore, it would stand to reason that the major focus of the SPHR exam is in Management Practices.

**Q. -** **Are the questions different between the PHR and SPHR examinations?**

**A. -** Yes. PHR questions tend to be technical and operational. They involve the cognitive abilities of recall and comprehension. The SPHR questions tend to be more policy oriented and strategic. They test more of one's ability to analyze and synthesize, often using scenario questions.

**Q. -** **What is a scenario question?**

A. -   A scenario question includes a paragraph (called an information set) which provides basic information about a given situation. It is followed by a series of four answer multiple choice items. Scenario questions are ideal for SPHR examinations because they require the examinee to integrate information from more than one functional area of the HRCI Content Outline to arrive at a correct answer. Scenario items reflect situations commonly encountered by senior level HR practitioners.

Q. -   **Do I have to memorize what year a law was passed?**

A. -   HRCI examinations do not test over trivia! For instance, it's not important to know what year (1935) the Wagner Act was passed. But you should know how to identify an employer unfair labor practice. Remember HRCI examination questions are very practical and are applied.

Q. -   **If I don't know the answer to a question should I leave it blank?**

A. -   No! Scoring is based upon the number of correct answers. A guess is far better than leaving a question blank.

Q. -   **I have heard from past examinees that there are far more training and development questions on the examination than the weightings on the HRCI content outline would indicate. How can that be?**

A. -   It just appears that way. HRCI examinations are weighted precisely to the weightings included on the HRCI Content Outline. In the training and development area there aren't a lot of alternative words as in other sections of the outline. As a result, the words "training" and/or "development" appear quite often either in the stem or options of a question. This gives the impression of more training and development questions compared to other areas of the examination. In reality, the weighting on the outline is correct.

Examination Administration

Q. - **What happens if you are unable to get to your test center due to inclement weather on test day?**

A. - Notify the HRCI test vendor within three (3) days following the examination date to be eligible for a refund or to reschedule.

Q. - **I have a disability. Can accommodations be made for me at the examination site?**

A. - The HRCI certification examination program complies with the American With Disabilities Act regulations covering both facilities and administration. If you need special accommodations, submit a request with supporting documentation to the HRCI test vendor at the time you submit your application. The Certification Information Handbook describes these procedures.

Q. - **What if my religion precludes me from Saturday testing?**

A. - There are special procedures for non-Saturday test administrations including a written request supported by documentation from a clergy member or religious leader. Check your Certification Information Handbook.

Q. - **Do I need a calculator to take the examination?**

A. - Examination questions are designed to be answered without the aid of calculators. Check the most recent Certification Information Handbook to find out whether they may be used.

Q. -    **What should I do if I fail?**

A. -    Start by reviewing your score report. In cases where an examinee fails, it will include the raw scores (number correct) for each of the six functional areas. This should serve as a road map to help you identify your weak areas so you can focus your additional preparation.

Q. -    **Can I have my examination rescored if I do not pass?**

A. -    As a routine practice, examination score sheets which fall within two or three points on either side of the passing score are automatically rescored by hand. In all the years that HRCI has been administering examinations, it has never encountered a scoring error. If your examination score was not within a couple of points of the passing score and you still want a hand score, it can be arranged for a supplemental fee. See the applicable Certification Information Handbook for details.

Q. -    **Can I request to review my test booklet or get a list of the questions I missed?**

A. -    Because of test security, test booklets and questions/answers can not be made available for review. If you have questions regarding your examination, you should direct them in writing to the HRCI examination vendor at the address in the Certification Information Handbook. All inquiries are reviewed.

Recertification

Q. -    **How do I recertify?**

A. -    Recertification is required every three years by the expiration date of current certification cycle. Recertification can be achieved by:

- Successfully retesting
   or
- Documenting 60 contact hours of activities that update ones HR knowledge and/or experience

Q. - **What education and experience counts toward the 60 contact hours needed for recertification?**

A. - Activities in the following categories can count toward recertification:

| | |
|---|---|
| Continuing Education (Seminars, workshops, conferences) | 60 hours |
| Research and/or Publishing | 20 hours maximum |
| Instruction | 20 hours maximum |
| On the-Job Projects | 10 hours maximum |
| HR Leadership | 10 hours maximum |
| Professional Membership | 10 hours maximum |

Contact HRCI for a Recertification Application.

Q. - **Where did the three year time frame come from for recertification?**

A. - A recognition by the HRCI Board of the amount and speed of change occurring in the HR field.

Q. - **Why did HRCI do away with lifetime certification for SPHR's?**

A. - The HRCI Board did away with lifetime certification for SPHR's in recognition of the dynamic changes in the HR field. The HRCI Board saw that HR practitioners must constantly keep abreast of changing laws and new developments in the field. The HRCI Codification Process provided the Board an indication of the magnitude of these changes. Technical obsolescence comes quickly in the HR field. Lifetime certification did not reflect the realities of today and was eliminated. Those who had already held lifetime certification were grandfathered. Beginning in 1996 and thereafter, newly certified individuals will have to recertify every three(3) years.